Upon This Stoney Holy Year

James Timberlake

authorHOUSE®

AuthorHouse™
1663 Liberty Drive
Bloomington, IN 47403
www.authorhouse.com
Phone: 1-800-839-8640

© *2011 James Timberlake. All rights reserved.*

No part of this book may be reproduced, stored in a retrieval system, or transmitted by any means without the written permission of the author.

First published by AuthorHouse 8/31/2011

ISBN: 978-1-4634-3946-0 (sc)
ISBN: 978-1-4634-3947-7 (e)
ISBN: 978-1-4634-3948-4 (hc)

Library of Congress Control Number: 2011913587

Printed in the United States of America

Any people depicted in stock imagery provided by Thinkstock are models, and such images are being used for illustrative purposes only.
Certain stock imagery © Thinkstock.

This book is printed on acid-free paper.

Because of the dynamic nature of the Internet, any web addresses or links contained in this book may have changed since publication and may no longer be valid. The views expressed in this work are solely those of the author and do not necessarily reflect the views of the publisher, and the publisher hereby disclaims any responsibility for them.

To Bodhidharma

cover photograph by James Timberlake
photographs from the journey at www.jimtimberlake.com
author photograph by Deb Hickey

poetry is the veil
that slows the swim of moments
into a meal.

James Timberlake

Introduction

In 2004 I made my first trek to Santiago de Compostela walking 1000 miles from Le-Puy-en-Velay in Southeastern France... and what a trip!

Years earlier, traveling through France in the manner I used to enjoy... a bus here, a train there, a hitchhike to the next town... By virtue of the towns I chose to visit I slowly became aware of a network of trails extending across the French countryside. The frequent question arose, "Are you a pilgrim?" "What?" My American mind tending toward Plymouth Rock, Black Capotain Hats and Big Buckled Shoes, but soon the awareness grew to encompass le Chemin de St. Jacques, el Camino de Santiago, Jakobsweg, that is - The Way of St. James - a medieval pilgrimage comprised of long-distance footpaths leading to a Cathedral Shrine in faraway Galicia... a route that has threaded its way through 1000 years of European history, literature and mythology, and which still exists today... And I felt awareness become desire.

Knowing I can obsess about gathering information, I struggled to approach the Way with clear eyes. Yes, I sought out internet advice about what to bring with me but, not wanting to hold a list of things I should see in my head I let go of 'intellectual hoarding mind' and opened myself to the active experience of walking across France and Spain, of making my mistakes and learning from them, and of appreciating whatever appeared before me with zennist embrace and zennist letting-go.

The result is this book. While <u>Sons of Thunder</u> and <u>Autumn on the Trail to Santiago</u> celebrate a much longer journey spanning seasons and 2000 miles of trails, they also reflect the experience gained from having made the pilgrimage before. Having no prior knowledge, <u>Upon This Stoney Holy Year</u> is a simpler piece of work. There are no Formal E-mails, no Definitions, no Autobiography or Research here. And for all that it is not, this book completes those first two in the pilgrimage series in a gentle way.

6/20/2004

departure's eve,
    solstice light late in the sky,
        my favorite indigo
    winged in Milky Way immortal flight.

eyes flash east, west, east, up,
    one nightmared wren implodes with song,
        feathers sifting through amber streetlight beams,
    shadow at last kissing quill.

to feast at Casa Portugal
    before i leave this summering country,
        not returning home until bright-veined autumn leaves
    tide my den's gate.

bright-veined leaves and Orion high
    on the other side my departure tomorrow
        into so much unknown,
    the belly ripples with anticipation

walking home wine-stained lips,
    locks of garlicky grilled bacalhau wedge
        tasty aches between my teeth,
    and simply home for a narrowing span of hours ~

two flies in the room.
    one i captured in a yogurt cup and
        set night free. the other bangs
    lightbulb and geranium reflected black window glass.

wings wings wings rumbling,
    stale jet plane air will linger in the whiskers
        sprawled upon a firm foreign hotel mattress.
    foreign hotel toilet down the hall,
        i'll be eyeing that shallow bedside sink.

journal - 6/22/04

uneventful flight. cool monitor screen on the back of the seat in front of me. meaty golfing businessman to the right kept resting elbow on my Volume control... to the left, an old woman who got a nosebleed on the descent.

Terminal 4. BA360... Gate not yet posted.

Lyon didn't appear too attractive. a busy, dirty, modern city... if i get back here by the 12th of October: bus / train / metro transfer station Lyon Part Dieu and stay in the nearby two-star 'Athens' hotel. from there i can grab the airport shuttle for 8.5E - leaves every 20 minutes.

6/22/2004

banking west to align with Heathrow runway ways,
    quick dawn sun melts
        phantasmagoric shadows
            across cabin ceiling storage bins.

stale-eyed airport morning.
    Dad would have loved the in-flight GPS monitor screen
        tracking altitude, ground speed, exterior temp.,
  time and miles left to land,
      and the cartoon icon plane's skate
        across the sea.

eating sweet flesh cherries
    and a hard-boiled egg my Mom packed,
      goodbye card i bought for
        a dying uncle
           falls
      from
    the new journal not
      two pages broached.

6/22/2004

yellowest ever
    hard-boiled
        yolk
in stillness steals
    my bite-print. waiting.

Heathrow ventilation
        thunder maddens
Heathrow walls.

my body
    in 3:am daylight
        begins sour
            disjointed
        descent
    to firm French
        hotel bed.
            waiting.

6/22/2004

last stage to Le Puy ~
    nodded a knot in the neck
        on this rackety train napping,
            unbolted metal cabinet doors hiding
                'mechanisms'
    bang open.
wide-eyed dog fear, tail curlicues tiny balls beneath master's seat.
    now, St. Étienne Châteaucreux station cables
        in crazed suspension bridge spans
            hum wind, bead rain.
                waiting.
        European ambulance strangely wails.

journal - 6/23/04

met a couple other pilgrims on the train. easily affable René, slowing his elocution and speaking clearly for me. Deiter's French - none. René's German - a little. but we made out fine. interesting how humor comes through with so few words. i was going to grab the first cheap hotel i came across and crash but instead, following René's historic knowledge, the three of us made our way up to Le Grand Séminaire du Puy and got rooms.

next morning, entering the Cathedral for the 7:am Pilgrim's Mass sending walkers on their way as has been the way for nearly 1000 years - pretty grey-habited nun asks us to bring the bread and wine up to the altar. later at the statue of St. Jacques we received the Bishop's blessing. candlelight, shadow, and incensed stone walls.

about 15 pilgrims formed a semicircle there, and before benedictory formalities the Bishop went around and asked our origination. he was well-travelled and had a congenial something to say about everyone's home or as close to that home as he had been. told me he had a sister in NYC and when he visits they eat at the Bar Breton on Fifth Avenue. after the blessing there was a Latin chant to the Black Madonna of Le Puy and we were each given a silver medallion with her image embossed upon the back... then to the Sacristy to have our credentials stamped and receive iconic scallop shells. that the stamp is called a 'tampon' in French makes most Anglos chuckle.

with handshakes, waves and good wishes Deiter rode off on his saddlebag laden bike, René on foot, and i went straight back up to bed in my seminary cell as i'm not leaving until tomorrow.

it was emotive to take part in an ancient tradition - for centuries pilgrims have gathered and been blessed there. the video presentation in the Sacristy calls the benediction scene a 'living and ancient fresco... the steps we take, like serpent's scales falling away, renewing ourselves to ourselves.'

after the nap - practicalities - phone card / maps / Petit Casino grocery. visited St. Michel d'Aiguilhe sitting atop a near 300-foot basalt needle - the hard lava core that remains after the outer volcano has eroded away. these outcroppings populate the Auvergne and have been sacred places since prehistory. mythologically, the first one to officially make the pilgrimage from these parts - the Bishop of Le Puy - built this chapel upon his return from St. Jacques de Compostelle. the Xth Century structure itself is currently closed for renovations, but craning my neck through a hole in the fence i can see a giant fresco hand, which workers have uncovered above the door, held in the mudra of No Fear.

sat outside the chapel overlooking the city from the heights, the Cathedral, the towering Madonna and Child statue topping another nearby 'needle,' and the distant flat-topped volcanic mountain range. clouds sprinkle. everyone looks at me and says the same thing mounting the last of the 268 steps... "Whew!" the 'living and ancient fresco.' experiencing there the feeling of starting a long journey, dwelling in the point of departure and not return. this trek ending in Plum Village for some time of still meditation after walking 1000 miles to the sea.

René had a casual openness about him that has done much for letting my hesitation speaking French pass away, will try to retain this spirit.

15E equals about 19USD.

walked around trying to find places i visited six years ago... the pizzeria on the main drag across from City Hall was closed. the night i ate there City Hall Plaza erupted with Bastille Day fireworks! i found the spiral-staircased restaurant where i feasted on trout stuffed with green lentils - the famous lentilles vertes du Puy! ...and the little Brit kid yelling down the spiral stairs, "Can I come downstairs, Daddy? Daddy, can I come downstairs? Can

I come downstairs, Daddy? Daddy, can I come downstairs?" over and over and over in pendulous repetition finally snapping his Mom's last nerve who shouted out unexpectedly to the crowd, (and even to herself), "QUIET! HE'S GONE TO COP A PEE!"

6/23/2004

chef joining Aznavour
        refraining 'la Bohème' in the back room...
    salad, lentils, sausage, wine,
        five fist-sized purple allium
        from a murk water glass vase bloom,
    transubstantiate, become tomorrow's alpha
beginning so much of sweat and miles.

seminary courtyard chestnut
        trees, the nightlong,
        rustle streamly deep corners
            of room and soul.

journal - 6/24/04

walking out of Le Puy an older man with kind eyes asked me if i was going all the way to Compostelle. 'Finisterre, actually.' he said it is tradition to burn one's clothes there. 'What? And get on the plane home nude? Maybe I'll just burn my socks.' laughing, he wished me well.

the Chemin follows the GR65, (Grande Randonnée - the long-distance hiking trails that web the French countryside), and it changed modes many times - crushed rock - dirt track - narrow paved lanes through small stone communities - some crumbling, some with lighter new mortar seams. everything stone looks old. everything stone is old. people get all rapt over a 300-year-old tree while the pebble in their palm has seen five million summers. agriculture first - wheat, hay, corn - later more husbandry. apparently there are several famous, (and by that i assume the French mean 'tasty'), bovine breeds in the Auvergne.

for stumbling rods and cones i stepped slowly into an XIth Century village church and from the dark interior, "Bonjour Pèlerin!" five or six people appear. some in biking attire. some in street clothes. they all seemed to know each other. the litany of friendly questions… where am i from? where did i start? how long did it take? how far am i going today? how much does my pack weigh?

the village water fountain flashes with stippled trout, the brown goat herd grazing, a huddle of wide-eyed kittens - stock-still - watching an early morning pilgrim passing by. woman wearing a bright blue apron in her yard with such thick green grass begging to be toe-sunk, she's snipping stringbeans into an enamel bowl. the jet black dog of Monbonnet who wanted to shake paws and up on his hind legs thumping my chest to be pet.

from there started the steady rise up les Monts du Devès. wildflowers colorfully constellate everywhere. they used to be distant blue, these heights - now their firs shade the trail. rough grey lichens overtaking stone, Queen Anne's Lace, and the broom i love so much in yellow bloom. long descent, the broad track becoming a narrow jumble of stones - rough on blistered feet… and then to the gîte in St. Privat. laughed with my long-bearded roommate about the sign back in Le Puy indicating 5H45M to St. Privat… it took me 7H and him somewhat more.

stone homes and bright shutters. XIIth Century chapel on the outcrop overlooking the gorge. long conversation with an old guy who stopped strolling his walker by a flourishing honeysuckle to talk.

6/24/2004

    after pilgrim's mass,
        Le Puy Bishop's blessing
            by the statue of St. James.
he, a few slow kind words
        after each spoke their place of origination,
    often lost in old Cathedral stone echoes,
        but what is breathed kind remains...
    candles flicker into stillness
        as centuries of wax-wick flame
            have here
    before the Road to Santiago's
        fears and joys and pains express soul sweat flesh.

from much mind wandering and wondering how...
        wind and incense spark now's lips.
these early morning cobblestone steps,
    walking stick ticking beside me,
        dawn behind.

6/24/2004

about the hour when today's pilgrims
    receive the Bishop's blessing ~

my footsteps on volcanic stone,
    whiskered wheat,
        knee-high green corn,
    backpack straps creak,
        walking stick metronome.
            behind Rugosa rose cascades
meadows rise with cricket and birdsong
    until midday sun silence.

red crêpe petal poppy nods,
    waymarker giggles 1,521K
        to Compostelle.

6/24/2004

yellow and pink
　　wildflower stars,
　　　　white cones,
　　purple spears among lichened stone,
breakfast cartoon cereal laughs back at me
　　　　from the poem's page.

6/24/2004

crossing
　　les Monts du Devès range crest,
　　a field of gold-flame-bloom broom burns wind...
when white butterfly bursts from purple thistle,
　　　　i always thought it was a
　　　　　　clockmaker's dream...
a flesh, blood, and hollow-boned cuckoo
　　calls out a crazed 35 o'clock.

journal - 6/25/04

had a French breakfast, (coffee in a bowl, bread-butter-jam), with
the Two Gentilshommes hiking a nine-day circuit. the gorge
opposite the gîte was churning full with morning vapor. got
stamped and took off.

in the shadow of Rochegude's crumbling and precariously clung
tower, the Two Gentilshommes showing me the black cross in a
wild poppy's center... Augustinian Christians seeking signs and
meanings. missed a balise, walked awry, and later met up with
the Two again, and a young Parisienne. they chided me, "Vous
n'avez pas encore le nez," the 'nose' for the Chemin, and they're

right. there is always a balise at an intersection or bifurcation and my perception is not yet honed.

we walked together for a while as a quartet, then left the Two behind. long thigh burning descent to Monistrol-d'Allier, and the ceaseless back-knotting ascent up from the river, sweltering at 10:30. step after step and space falls away below.

cedar forest. tomato, prune, apple, cheese, hard-boiled egg and pastry lunch on a needle softened stone. fortunately the trail didn't redescend and Saugues is somewhere ahead on this plain. continued on through several hamlets - stone and crude timber, tractors haying... strangely, sometimes the wind blows chill.

missed another balise. coming towards me a 1/4 mile away on the path, a shepherd starts waving hands and staff and i'm thinking 'shit he doesn't want me near his sheep.' then faintly on the wind... "est là-haut, le Chemin!" 'the trail's over there!'

missed that balise and had to walk an extra mile up to the GR65's descent into Saugues. this region is home to the Bête de Gévaudan legend - probably a large wolf, or my thought is an early serial killer tearing apart lone women and children in the fields. so the saying goes, "When twigs crack, don't whistle."

beautiful day, blue skies over hamleted plains and pain. blisters under the big toe and balls of the feet, calves spasm and cramp, forearms sunburned, heat-rashed groin, the brow aching from continual squint-smiling because this. is. so. awesome!

will spend two nights here. my body needs a staggered start to snap into shape.

8:45pm - still light. walked, rather, hobbled my Aleve-ridden frame around town. by the little things one sees - carvings, pictures, statuettes - i'm realizing this region is known for its snails and mushrooms.

6/25/2004

another river to ridge climbed,
  sweat dries in cricket cedar breeze.
 soon these peaks too will turn
   hinter distance smokey blue
    and vanish.

6/25/2004

volcanic pumice to granite ~
 stone and cricket change dharma
  under horizon-bridged
  cloud front floes.
gargantuan hare i took for a lithe deer jacks ass away.
  acrid waft, Gauloise
   smoking fat old dude in working
man's blues... if you gotta toil,
  wear the Queen of Heaven's hue.
   sun-roasted horse-shit incenses its way
    back to a pile of hay.

journal - 6/26/04

restful day. mailed back some weight, mailed Dad a couple maps so he can follow me from home, picked up fruit and cheese for lunch, picked up a tube of cream at the pharmacy for the heat rash.

everyone is watching the EuroFoot games.

a slow stroll out of town and up to the snarling block-wood carving
of the Bête de Gévaudan to watch our sun set behind the towered
town, turning blue, and cows chaw.

6/26/2004

    fieldstones
        backbreakingly labored into Saugues' homes
        well before my time,
    tranquil under shine blue skies ~
the soothing screech of swallow skeins whirling
        knit and purl long memories to
    rock   meadow   mind.

6/26/2004

swallows sing daylight hamlet walls,
    dogs bay night fields,
stuff-sacked gear strewn about
    a resting room.

6/26/2004

dusty violet forget-me-nots in
    buttercup embrace

blue cornflowers ring around the
    yellow blooming broom bush

no idea the name indigo
    tangles no idea the name gold

between crystal azur sky and
    field green,
how nature joys in caressing
    the center of light's spectrum
and toppling expectation
    with one white crow.

6/26/2004

sometimes, so
    little in
        beauty.
    patchwork fields
        roll with subtle
    shifting shades,
a ring of fir fringes the meadow's bowl
    for scalloped
        clouds to
            to drift in,
        whose
    axis is
        one
    wild pink rose.

6/26/2004

apricot blazed
    western Auvergne sky,
        walking from hilltop bench
           to hamlet hollow,
    the horizon-wide cloud gyre...
titan crashes to sea and dies.

journal - 6/27/04

this morning i met steps with a Québecois couple who love Old Orchard Beach! they're doing the Chemin in sections walking yearly 10 days at a time. and i bumped into Chloe from St. Privat. easy walking... rolling and slightly rising. long hot stretch after meeting with a couple French guys Chloe knew. strange sensation - as the day wore on, and as the more tired i got, the less i understood of French and the less i could speak.

Chapelle de St. Roch - such cold springwater refreshes me washing down bread, tomato, cheese and figs. so much of broom in bloom along the stonewall-lined path. Chloe and the others turned off later to the village of la Roch where they'd heard of a private gîte with good food.

hot but pleasant descent into Saint-Alban-sur-Limagnole - the hills behind, fields opening below - old guy in blue overalls, "Il faut un chapeau aujourd'hui, eh?" goddamned right. woman i passed several times with casual hellos back in Le Puy is at the gîte. woke her up while unpacking. French. Monique. she convinced me to mail back my tent. even if the gîtes are full she says people sleep on the floor on extra mattresses. it's not worth the weight. she also suggested Compede for the blisters.

not much to Saint-Alban. gîte dorm is in the bare-beam attic of an old hotel. will eat the hotel demi-pension with the veloist, Monique, and an Amiable German Couple i passed earlier in the day. bumped into the guy in the church - didn't recognize him at first unbackpacked. he seemed taken by the pillar carving of a 'sirène,' a mermaid, with two tails.

together we enjoyed soupe aux cèpes, blanquette de veau with cabbage and pasta, cheese, and a baked apple with crème anglaise...

6/27/2004

early morning
   hostel already empty ~
      waiting for the pharmacy to open
      to bandage bleeding feet ~
   swallows spin spontaneous roller coaster courses
      around age-melted stone church walls ~
         yellow wildflower tuft eking it out
            in the saint-strolled eaves...
   geraniums glow with within light the overcast allows.

journal - 6/28/04

Monday morning. walked out of St. Alban and into a few showers, which upped the humidity, but i love heat and humidity. mostly a white gravel path through woods and high pastures, auburn cattle surrounded by pine and broom, rolling hazy distance. there's the frequent scene of blue cornflowers quivering in a field of green wheat stalks that is dizzying to look into.

strolling back from the church in Aumont-Aubrac - Chloe, Claire, Alain and Jacques were entering the gîte. we're all sharing the room... Alain and Jacques had everyone in stitches while screwing with their cell phones trying to program each others' home-phone numbers, but instead unintentionally calling other friends like two old coots befuddled in the modern world. Alain had me in tears again when he yelled at the cat, "Sac-à-Puce! Dégage!" and Jacques when the 'fly that broke the Frenchman's back' landed on his leg,

again! exasperates, "Ben Putain Mouche, Alors!" sometimes it's
just how the words hit you.

the ritual: bathe, handwash clothes, attend to feet, attend to food,
evening stroll around a quiet town.

Alain says tomorrow's walk is a wonder.

that second skin is a wonder - the whole plaster adheres to the blister
all day. didn't feel a thing from those four hotspots. Compede!
thank you Monique!

6/28/2004

ten minutes rain,
     ten minutes repose in
          cedar whisper,
birdsong rises with spectral vapour to the blue,
     smelling horse-shit brings me back
          a thousand years to now.

6/28/2004

     white limestone track winds
esses through rolling plateaux,
     stunningly one auburn bovine tucked in
          pine and yellow broom relief
               grinds her cud.
one twilight blue cornflower among
     infinite wicks of straight green wheat,
          the quivering-in-stillness
               entrances.
     red-white barred fence post balise beacons on.

6/28/2004

my belly full of beets and eggs,
       homecooked meal in foreign land.
    stretching back to make more room for
         contentment,
      black mote swallows swirl
        against avalanching clouds.
two-minded farm cat at my feet staring...
    raptures to my fingers,
    wishes he had wings.

a prayer in l'église St. Étienne-d'Aumont-Aubrac...

que rien ne te trouble,
    que rien ne t'effraie,
       tout passe.
dieu ne change pas.
    la patience obtient tout,
      celui qui a dieu
ne manque de rien.
    dieu seul suffit.

journal - 6/29/04

slept well, woke well - the room emptied. fruit and cheese in the kitchen. got the tampon and was offered a congenial cup of coffee 'to help me on my way.' walked out of town eating my oven-warm baguette. passed through a few hamlets... chickens running away from me on the horseshoe-printed track. met up with Chloe, Alain and Jacques, and shared a switchblade sliced and tooth-torn pilgrim's lunch by a masoned spring - they, good-naturedly arguing over the varied pronunciations from their disparate regions. AND THEN the Aubrac opened up.

crossing high volcanic plateaux through stonewall channels lined with broom and gentiane rolling... through the deserted village with a 'travail,' a large frame-brace used to restrain a horse being shod or castrated... and into Nasbinal - private gîte... bathed, laundered, foot care.

coming back from the grocery, Chloe, Alain and Jacques at the bar! had a beer with them, then the Québecois walked by and snap! an instant party! want a party? add two Québecois and stir. as they talked, the Q and Alain realized they had a common friend in the universe. on the trail last year Alain was the one who helped this 'mutual' after she passed out from heat exhaustion. when she awoke there was an orphan puppy by her side and she named him 'Camino.' Camino followed her to all the way to Santiago and she has him still!

6/29/04

crisp village morning,
    crackt open baguette end steams.
        breath vapour hangs dew in
           whiskers,
      glistens fields...
    walking into birdsong.

6/29/2004

country road
    cricket field
        birdsong pines,
  one sapphire-eyed black butterfly
      guides me five steps
        along the way.

6/29/2004

sudden as sunrise,
        a door opens, or glass breaks...
top of the world Aubrac plateau rolls away
            to belittled blue
            mountains round,
heaven here and heaven now silvery green pastures
        spangled with gentiane, daisy,
    broom, and cowbells graze...
            long summer light in fieldstone stonewalls
                still warm well into
                    starry hours.

journal - 6/30/04

met the Québecoise at the bar in the morning and helped her with her glasses. she lost a screw. i had one in my kit, but not the bolt... used my dental floss as thread and she chuckled how minty fresh she was. we got stamped and made our way out.

fewer stonewalls. more unlocking and locking of cattle gates. out of all this wide-open space a contentious brawn bull decided to plop down on the trail itself, bodily blocking the one gate through. and the slapstick scene of us clambering backpacks and walking sticks over an electric-fenced stonewall - laughter and shocked thigh hollers under broad skies!

village of Aubrac - peeked in the café / restaurant - an at least! two-foot-wide fruit tart cooling, unattended... hobo-ic temptations racing blood.

St. Chély. stone homes and geraniums tucked to the side of a mountain. an upper-storied gîte - attic rooms. will sleep well here.

i can smell it, that depth of rest. have been attempting afternoon vipassana and breathing meditation in the local church but i keep toppling over to the left, falling asleep.

two Frenchwomen, Chloe, and Alain and Jacques. cooking with them i learned the verb meaning to soften onions in a pan is 'revenir.' my "Où sont-ils allés qu'ils doivent revenir" got the loudest unintentional laugh.

Jacques - after joking about how he leapt over the wall from the bull says, "Prévenir vaut mieux que guérir." 'better to anticipate than to heal' - or actually - 'an ounce of prevention is worth a pound of cure.' he likes his sayings as much as Yves Montand's old man Soubeyran.

caught a video at the tourist office with Chloe, Alain and Jacques. they've been playing the same VCR tape for 20 years. great old footage of the incredible snowfalls in the Aubrac - of the tremendous winds and drifting, the lone stone-hovelled isolation, the flower bursts of Spring - swinging specially made rakes gathering jonquil flowers, harvesting the gentiane root with long-tined pitchforks to brew into the local apéritif, the pagan procession of cattle wearing huge bells and towering flowered headdresses up to these high pastures to graze on wild grasses and herbs all spring and summer making their Fall meat renowned... the milking, the cheese-making process... l'aligot - the tomme cheese beaten with potato and garlic until elastic-y. in restaurants it's often drawn up from a vat tableside and scissor-snipped onto the plate.

the poor German women in my room, they left St. Chély this morning and confused the GR6 with the GR65 and did about 40K... all to circle back to St. Chély at the end of the day... ouch.

18 | James Timberlake

6/30/2004

    butterfly alights,
        black velour wings pulse
            tucking a cricket into
each hatred and
    fear...
        beechwood leaf shadows
            gently knead the ground.

6/30/2004

knee-high stonewalls cling a tree-tunneled path
    to steep Aubrac mountainsides,
        these thousand-year-old eyes...
sweet scent of hot valley hay rising ~
    St. Chély hamlet bar,
        cold beer in cold glass,
            lucky bamboo coils in
    a stoney cobalt bowl.

journal - 7/1/04

the German women slept so well! the French crew started off earlier as usual. i had a hearty breakfast at the gîte then headed out through the village. overcast, switchbacks - saw where the Germans made their mistake.

the wooded trail descended all day, clung to steep escarpments.

i was attacked by three dogs! fended them off with the walking stick, my back sliding across the stonewall behind me, and made it down to Saint-Côme-d'Olt... to Alain's house - a second simple country house his wife can't stand... crumbling, pigeons overtaking the upper rooms, front patio embraced in wide wisteria wings and linden tree shade.

he jumpstarted his rickety jeep and we took a pell mell ride through narrow streets and moguled dirt roads to rest by the rushing river Lot. went back to town and took a tour. Alain knew everyone... visited St. Côme's famed flèche flammée, the church's 'coiled' steeple rising above town. a rarity. only about 30 of this style still exist in France. and he explained the 'soleil,' a wild artichoke type of barometer - when it's going to rain it closes up. when it's dead, dried and splayed out it makes like a cool piece of weathered 'driftwood' to nail to a barn wall or over a door.

butcher shop. apéritifs. fried onions and king-size steaks of Auvergne beef into a feast with l'aligot, wine, and what warmth to wander, then suddenly be nestled in a home.

7/1/2004

roosters, chickens, trough water trickling
    from a pipe hammered into mountain stone.
        the wide-eyed goat bleats and shits black beads.
    vvvvvvvvvvvvvvvvvvvvvvvvv
    vvvvvvvvvvvvvvvvvvvvvvvvvvv
        wild rosebush bees, invisible lizard
scuttles under leaves. one calf, snout to hooves,
        snores calf dreams against mother's thigh...
            these thousand-year-old eyes.
no matter which way
        the breeze blows y'always get
            a whiff of your own wind.

journal - 7/2/04

it took the longest time leaving the village. Alain stopped and was stopped by everyone! told Jacques we should get him horse blinders. separated from them soon thereafter as i wanted to walk the trails, and they, the more direct inter-village lanes for the less upping and downing.

market day in Espalion. took a photo of a steaming deep and six-foot-wide pan of paella they're scooping up and selling by the quart, er, liter. i love walking from the scent of a forest into the scent and bustle of a market day. at the end of the town, sitting in the grass with her head in her hands - Chloe. trouble with her recent exams. she was going to bag the Chemin and return home. frustrated, but recovering quickly back to her Parisian 'c'est la vie' style.

Estaing was impressive, carved out of the forest, massive stone fortress in the town center and flowering cascades down banisters everywhere. walked a long quiet road by the river Lot, then switchbacked endlessly up...

met up with Alain and Jacques here in the Golinhac gîte - Jacques shouting down the hallway to the Québecois, "Jeem est là! Jeem est là!" and the Q's "ooo oooooo" handshakes and kisses. the unphotographable richness of recognition, the brother/sisterhood of walking the Way.

Alain said Golinhac is only 20 years old, looks it. new gîte. great shower. must be a station for hikers and bikers and campers, o my. my sunset bench overlooking high here and distant patchwork hilltop fields...

7/2/2004

leaving Saint-Côme-d'Olt,
    a ferrous red stone path through
        green woods winds,
wild mint and chestnut catkin blooms
    incense crisp morning air.
        with the trail's novelty gone
mind turns to vicious 'should have and will'
    internal repartée, sometimes saved
        by a cowbell or raspberry thorned thigh
          bleeds.

journal - 7/4/04

walked long with the Québecois yesterday morning. Alain and Jacques, (of course), left earlier. Espeyrac - we found Monique's handwriting in a church guest book, which serves also as a communication log among the pilgrims. and her script again in Senergues where the Q stopped for coffee.

on paths wide and narrow, through pines and broad fields - rerouted Pierre, a randonneur oddly adrift with a white umbrella. the approach of two dogs... Pierre backing away "oh Oh OH," but if they're not barking you're safe. extended hand and they were satisfied with a few sniffs... just wanted to know who was passing by their home. Chapelle St. Marcel's stained glass scallop shells and welcoming open door juxtapose the braying donkey who seriously wanted to chomp off my arm.

steep descent into Conques tucked against a hillside. a town of ochre stone, black slate roofs, narrow streets, and geranium spills. the people with the severely wounded feet from Golinhac are here at the gîte, smiling all the same. met up with Alain and Jacques for a beer. the Québecois passed by and sat down for a frothy sustenance as well. they're all staying at the Abbey. the Code by the Abbey in the Guide is P.O. - "participation obligatoire." just as it sounds - and i didn't feel like praying. we talked about the Chemin in Spain - el Camino. yellow arrows mark the trail there, not the red and white balises. they instructed me to go directly to the Pilgrim's Office in Santiago and register so i'd be counted among those present at Mass the next morning. long storied myth about a falsely accused itinerant pilgrim being hanged from a steeple, and roasted chickens leaping up from their serving platters proclaiming his innocence in a town called Santo Domingo de la Calzada - i'll get the scoop when i get there.

as attractive as Conques is, (one of 'The Most Beautiful Villages in France'), it's an architectural museum of bars, restaurants, and shops selling regional fare... but if a town doesn't even have a grocery there's something not real about it.

attended the latenight illumination in the church with organ music reverberating the amber glowing limestone walls.

slept well. woke with Wounded Feet and helped them to the pick-up point with their luggage. i guess a van is carrying their bags and they're walking light.

stayed in town for a rest day. strolled and napped and coffee and crêpes and ice cream and postcards.

the round-a-bout German women are here at the gîte... mice across the stone roof startled us from our nap. ran into Sonya from the blessing in Le Puy. those who walked today all comment on the heat.

7/4/2004

hot white gravel track,
    scintillant wings pulse butterfly-morse
        to blue dome skies.
across a steep ravine
        invisible jackass laughter echoes
            moon clear mind.

7/4/2004

at rest in Conques,
    afternoon stillness,
        fly wings' little breeze.

honey-oaken linden bloom scent
    bridges hat-tilt-eyed time until
        daydreams cloud the brim...

...dreaming warmly, darkly, wombly,
    a stonewall and boxwood tunnel
        warrens through steep forests.

over the next ridge
    lime-gold catkined chestnut groves
        ribbon down mountainsides.

swallow flocks juke one-mindedly
    and burst doppler song round
        stone Cathedral towers.

sudden sounds! small paws scrambling
    slate roof, six eyes popping wide.
        once sleeping strangers smile
            and check baguettes for signs.

7/4/2004

no cutting board
   in the gîte kitchen chasing
      chopping garlic round a flowered plate.
   knife clanks,
Cathedral gonging six o'clock
   quakes linden pollen off
      across-the-valley trees,
  wondering who might be below
      breathing by that honey-scented stream...
         hot butter bubbling in a banged up pan.

flights, flocks, volleys, sprays,
     formations, strays ~
glee squealing swallow silhouettes
    speckle sunset radiant Cathedral facade,
      soon sinking into early valley
        shadow.

    to be Swallow spirit here
     in eternal
       regeneration!

journal - 7/5/04

couldn't see the postcard view of Conques from across the gorge
for the blinding sunrise.

came across an older Frenchman sitting under a tree - didn't know
the word for 'cesspool' but asked him if he survived his passage by
the 'swimming pool of shit?' (if i don't know a word usually i can
describe it.) his face twisted up into 'oooo la laaa!' and we cracked
up. it was horrible. must serve to store manure for later use in the
fields, but presently - oooo la laaa!

that short sandy trail was the most scenic part of the day. arrival into compact Livinhac-le-Haut - everything closed up tight except for the Mairie's secretary office - payed, got stamped. i'm in cross-eyed nauseatic pain right now after putting baking soda on my heat-rashed groin. every time i move the powder falls into a new flesh fissure and the pain flares up again.

i seem to have stopped trembling. will try to make it to the shower and wash this stuff off. what a stupid idea thinking it would be like talc.

spent a social night out on the porch. everyone loved my multilayered sandwich. i'm appreciative of all things cultural, but the European style of sandwich with one slice of ham and one slice of cheese is useless. Sonya showed up... later, three Portuguese cyclists... fala fala fala... brain cramp trying to follow three languages.

7/5/2004

early morning
    leaving Conques,
one horny wren warbling
        every note known to Aves
        tumbling off tree twig leaf
            brush and briar floods the trail.
    blood-hungering savage flies
        beat three times with the hard of the palm
            don't die!
    wind-knocked chestnut blooms
        shower yellow pollen down upon me
    breaking through fern bracken...
        a summit row of staring cows,
            storm wall clouds,
and i am vertigo-ed with butterflies scuttling through sere hays.

26 | James Timberlake

after a piss in bird-rich copse ~ looking down,
 the glans mimes
 hands to cheeks
 Munch's 'Scream'
 getting tucked back behind zipper 'n fly
and i feel the same. something ominous.
 depth-charge thunder booms distant valleys,
 rain spatters the gravel trail.

journal - 7/6/04

more simple countrysides today. many useless 'virages,' zigzaggings
around private properties, hamlets with junk piled homes, rabbits
and pigeons in pens, but even in the tumbledowns - always flowers.
two kids chasing kittens up a ladder into hay, old woman on
her balcony saying what a nice day it is to walk, old guy with a
slowly burning butt on his lip waves from his tractor, much abiding
lavender grown into gnarly trunks, Rottweiler Bull charges at me
from behind a thankfully! high gate. overcast, but the sun came out
for the descent into Figeac... met Pascal and Thom at the gîte.

Thomas made his Grandmother's 'poté' - lean salt pork, sausage,
potato, carrot, turnip, and cabbage all in the cocote minute,
(pressure cooker), for 20 minutes.

7/6/2004

road-strewn golden chestnut catkins,
 ass-crack rash afire,
 humidity builds.
 don't think the heightening sun'll
have strength enough to burn horizon storm
 clouds away.

through fields of corn
    and fields of fallow,
        duckling and serpent in the hay...
crickets reading dolce dolce dolce.

7/6/2004

sister scents
    of horse-
        shit and hay,
    swatting fly away
      i vanquish
        sun,
           bug
        remains.

7/6/2004

descending tarmac
      road into Figeac,
    one windshield-wacked
      butterfly
      throes
in the breakdown lane.

7/6/2004

on cobbled Figeac hill,
    high stone walls
      and steeple rise to
        scratch passing evening light ~

softly walking into stillness
   i am bathed as well as any Pharaoh
      in the purple silken honey balm of
         flowering wisteria vines.

journal - 7/7/04

beautiful trails to Carjac - made up for the drab past two days.
wild plum and walnut trees. Thom said it was like the Midi here -
tough vegetation, dense-leaved oak trees, ratcheting cicadas.

had a beer at the same bar i sat at six years ago. familiar pale orange
and grey streaked cliffs in the distance.

7/7/2004

leaving Figeac by
   ancient Roman cobbleroads,
      between high stone walls
the early morning echo of
   six boots
      three walking sticks
and comfortable company silence...
tiny wild path-side plum
     sweetens teeth.

cicadas chisel the air...
   walking tree-tunneled trails,
      eyes of the world to me blind,
   night-black-maned maroon stallion
       grazes a patch of flaxen field.

7/7/2004

grey-blue
   stonewalls
      cleave
   red dirt path,
what odd god's giggle tucked
      in butterfly mind
         instincts insect
   to guide a man
      down this country
         trail,
walking west to meet the sea.

journal - 7/8/04

slept well in Cajarc, chilly morning, hot chocolate at le bar President. heated conversation at the counter about ... mushrooms!

one of the most beautiful days to my taste, wide paths through boxwood and oak, grey-blue stonewalls clotted with moss. took the wrong path - ass! found my way with compass and map but i added 1 1/2 hours to the walk.

Varaire. clean new gîte. not much here, an agricultural community... boarded up collapsing church, pigeon cock chasing pigeon hen around a tower ledge, grocery / gas station with shriveled vegetables.

damn cold - feels like October - dense clouds and now it rains. in our room - the smelly German, and the old man with Granddaughter and Grandson. for three years they've been doing a nine-day section of the Chemin - what gentle memories to form through

30 | James Timberlake

the years. showed the Grandson how to wrap a rubberband around
pinkie, thumb and index for precision flinging.

we three ate pasta with pesto and a lot of cheese. people speaking
too fast for me to comprehend. such concentration is tiring, and
after a day of physical exertion the foreign language quadrant in
the brain gets muddled.

7/8/2004

sitting on the shitter of the
        Carjac gîte,
    raw vegetable feast doing
        what
            it oughta ~
    window opens to
        bright grey-blue cliffs
            streaked powdery
                ochre and rose ~

mesmeric inattention.
    i'll have
        to
    scrub these
        fingernails.

7/8/2004

tight-leaved oak
        and boxwood limbs
    black with moss
            and early
        morning
            rain ~

between this red dirt path
    and streak of milky sky,
        feet
        eyes
        ears
        lips
        nose
        mind,
fruit, bread and cheese
    swinging in
        a shoulder bag.

7/8/2004

sudden cloud flight,
    oak shadow dappled
        path unrolls with a snap
           at the dusty boot's
             toe.
knapsack straps creak,
    turtledove sings in three-note time,
        wind hollows in wandering ears and
           dances orange crêpe
             paper
poppy clusters in blond wheat surround.
    when afternoon heat reaches
        trunken marrow
           cicada vibrations
        ratchet and rave.

7/8/2004

puff cloud rolling skies...
    a copse of trees in the meadow
        wreathes one lichened dolmen
            that has seen 100,000 summers.
hand to resonant stone,
    a dusty-booted man
        listens to cicadas
            in softly throbbing light.

7/8/2004

day's end.
    slick new gîte in
        one-horse hamlet,
    even the church is closed ⁓
familiar faces and strange gathering within
        foreign walls
            to feed and sleep and stable ⁓
joke with new friends about grabbing
    fists o' walkway lavender for the
        kindly old German stinking up our
        room ⁓
    down the hall, grandpère, petit-fils et -fille
        laugh across the kitchen table
            playing cards.
    and outside   900-year-old tower,
solid under coursing clouds and setting sun...
    the sapphire-maned pigeon cock
        nod nod nod nod chases
    pigeon hen round its crumbling
        ledge.

journal - 7/10/04

cold leaving Varaire yesterday morning. field of knee-high sunflowers facing east. started using foreseeable landmarks - upcoming stump, stone, limb, haybale, as meditation bells because i'm getting lost. be present just until that stump... until that dangling branch.

peaceful trails - heavy mist, nearly rain... clusters of purple clover, oak patches in meadows expand to forests, then i crossed the 'croupe' before descending into Cahors - always a descent into the village or town. sharp pain in the outer right knee ligaments - bought Musculor. smells like Tiger Balm. hoping one day of rest will help, but i doubt it.

met two guys from the Cajarc gîte about the same time as seeing Pascal and Thom on the street and had a good laugh! at various times today we all came across the SAME old codger in a village chattering his historic tidbits, we all heard the same stories. he must spend his day there.

palmier pastry down by the bridge after sleeping in this morning. click - everything changes again. Pascal and Thom continue on. wonder who'll be my walkmates this week?

entering Cathédrale St. Étienne - immediate scent i could not place but knew - old folks polishing pews with something that smells like pine pitch gum. simply carved cloister with a center of lavender and lilies, and a canopied market out on the Cathedral parvis. got a pizza with a melted slab of Cabeçou cheese and white asparagus. hearing a lot of Dutch and Brits, a few American voices.

siesta fissured by a carillon off the hour - wedding at St. Étienne must be getting out.

7/9/2004

low morning clouds,
　　hummingbirds flash
　　　mist-blurred
　　　　lavender patch ~
from the invisible,
　　one hawk peals,
　　　one human heart thrills.
companion bootsteps fade
　　　round a boxwood tunneled
　　　bend.

7/9/2004

sick of the most beautiful trail
　　　i kindly beat my mind
　　　with a stick ~
in silent bend between
　　field and oaks,
　　　smelling hot chocolate
　　　on the wind.

7/9/2004

broad shadow sunders into dappling light,
　　trail winds through hayfields...
　　　one side billowing,
　　　one side mown.
walking the green grass
　　between parallel cartwheel tracks
　　　softly, softly.

and in
    a rip of
        earth
    and sky,
   his back bent, shuffling two canes along,
     red-rimmed eyes,
laughing 'i'm 92 and a half, but they say i look only 80.'
  speaking like a faucet, me missing many words,
      'the tower now a pigeon house from
        gallo-roman times,
    the hundreds they buried
       during centuries of plague,
    the very road your walking
       via Pax Romana came.'
handshakes and salutations
     "santé! la santé, c'est tout!"

forgot to ask him the secret of longevity.
   forgot to ask him for his blessing.
      forgot to ask that he walk three steps with me
        down the trail.

churchbell gongs,
   the turtledove has always known
     the turtledove's song.

7/10/2004

along for the daylong ride,
    fat black gnats
       hover a handspan off
   the nose.
      lung and lip burst pfffft careens them
away a moment making footsteps steady,

then soon stumbling again...
    eyes cross finding foci so close.

7/10/2004

walking Cahors Cathedral cloister,
    an open dome of stillness above
    vaulted loggia ~ from four corners
        four paths lead to central
        sunlit lavender and white lily blooms
    untouched by morning breeze ~

and from over these sheltering walls,
    Saturday Cathedral square market scents
        delphicly arrive ~
        flowers, fruits, and
goat cheese towers, oregano bags and bags of thyme,
    children peddling mewling shoebox kittens,
        guitar and violin chanting gypsy rhymes,
and through an open oaken chapel door
    a couple elders polish pews
        and this memory of mine.

journal - 7/11/04

Sunday strolled and Sunday napped. hot chocolate here, beer there, everything is closed up. met Sonya in the bakery. she took a variante and said Rocamadour was incredible, carved into a cliff.

thinking of the day years ago when i left Cahors to walk to Saint-Cirq Lapopie... that day back then when i left Cahors to walk to Saint-Cirq Lapopie has changed my life. traveling as i used to - a bus here, a train there, a hitch as far as he/she wanted to take me - trying to hitch out of town, the road away from Cahors was busy and dangerous with transport trucks. said to myself, "Self, I wonder if there's a trail down by that river." tramping across private lands, figuring a hollering-at is better than ending up roadkill, and immediately upon the path, (that was indeed there), i met a Dutch woman walking the other way. she said some things about pilgrims and my American mind conceived black hats and turkey feathers.

my awareness soon expanded.

7/11/2004

another Cahors morning ~
    light gleams violet to golden
        through iron shutters sometimes
            banged by rising wind.

nail in the bone where neck becomes spine,
    knee ligament's strident cries,
        and temple heart-bells have begun
            to ring ~
        may horror not overtake he who
        finds my body cooling on
            the field of stars.

now, a few days without guiding red-white balise streaked
        stones and posts and walls
    i find me making pecking pigeon
        circles around town.

clicking a snapshot,
    toes to Pont Valentré's round cobblestones,
        tomorrow i'll cross this bridge
            and the River Lot,
    far and faintly
        cicadas
  beckon.

7/11/2004

an old wide wind
    rustles this grapevine, bamboo, and stone
        sheltered terrace,
  "a terrasse in the chade," says the restaurant sign.
smoked duck breast, goat cheese,
    and grilled aubergine terrine
        garnished with roasted pistachios
            and sweet flesh prune.
red snapper filets over
    ratatouille quilled with slivered garlic,
        parsley leaves pressed between shaved potato
            slivers and fried to vitrine translucence.
one fist-sized squash and three mushrooms stuffed
    with braised thyme-scented duck, three new potatoes,
        three roast tomatoes balance around
            a pool of jus.
    cherry/almond clafoutis and drizzled crème anglaise.

        and again a wind from the east blows mind
            to westerly seas.

journal - 7/12/04

hard day - pain and cold and rain.

7/12/2004

each step ~
    acid-splash knee joint tendons burn,
        shattered glass crams vertebrae.
wonder who hid all those well-whet nails
    round left lung, heart
        and shoulderblade.

bruised wedding petals stain
　　　the Cathedral's flagstoned square.
leaving Cahors,
　　　the cold and early morning rain.

　　　Spring wildflowers gone,
no smile or frown, all is simply living green ~

　　butterflies that once guided pilgrim steps
quiver with stilling death throes in low ground breezes,

　　or by ant mandibles are towed into wicked holes.
country churchbell rings the hour

　　　seeming more toll than time,
and even the flies leave my lunch alone.

one bumblebee hums round and round
　　one gnarly-boled chestnut tree,
　　　last month's map in apiarian mind...
　　now only thorny green burrs upon which to land.

journal - 7/13/04

left Lascabanes - fieldside stonewall and bramble growth to the left meet the overhanging forest to the right and make a tunneling flicker-lit trail. several trailside Welcome signs - 'cold drinks! sandwiches, shelter from sun and rain' - instead i was met by fierce dogs i had to beat back with my staff! trail descent into the Sunflower Valley, rows upon rows to the millionth, individually precise bloomage a stone's throw away to distance's yellow blur.

i was the first one at the gîte in Lauzerte, an outmoded old folks home - the elders having been relocated to a new facility down the road. bald Georges of the oooo la laaa cesspool showed up.

40　|　James Timberlake

the two Québecois! the Swisse who spent some time in Boston
and NYC, and Raymond from my room in Cahors. Lauzerte was
recently sandblasted and facelifted anew. had a beer on the sunny
main square watching cats with blue eyes prowl... the rolling
countrysides below extending outwards, tan wheat and sunflower
fields...

7/13/2004

fang-snapping mad farm dog froth
     still slicks
        walking staff.
   washing mind in
winded leaves, in the fiery sting nettles
   leave on calf and shin.

7/13/2004

crushed chalk track
   essing open hilltops,
     one black hole crow
       on the glean in
    platinum-blond cropped field,
from invisible hovering high above,
   sudden Pentecostal wren bursts out scales,
     twittering tongues
       the trail-long,
    saving me from thoughts each
French dog owner should be flogged
with the spiked leather leash he does not have.

7/13/2004

red cracked clay trail,
    tall tunneling oaks,
        a cicada for every overstrewn blue
    jigsaw puzzle piece of sky.

7/13/2004

Lauzerte rampart heights,
        back and ass against warm
    stone overlooking wide valley below ~
        patchwork tan, tilled, and green meadows
            fissured with poppling tree lines,
    sunflower field faces faintly yolken away.

bats and swallows juke black sparks upon
    deepening blue skies, falcon peals,
        bright sheep glean a close-cropped
            field, we all breathe the same
    cricket shimmer air.

invisible farmer burns trimmings into grey wisps,
    wind rises,
        dogs bay,
            the setting sun
        casts golden cloud shores
    a-hover in a sky golden sea.

nose burned in daylong communion,
    the stone ramparts dark.

journal - 7/14/04

left Lauzerte about 8:00. morning trails following open tarred and sycamore-lined lanes. crossed Raymond and the Swisse who took a photo of me in the sunflower sea, passed the three Françaises, Georges and the Québecois. ate another switchblade sliced and tooth-torn lunch with them in shady grass. passed two old farmers coming out of their barn piled high with garlic, flats of white papery bulbs in their arms... a pickup snails by and leaves a crate of melons in the woods with a jar beside to put trusting payment into... the scent of petrol exhaust and sweet musk.

descent into Moissac - ugly modern neighborhoods. staying at the Carmelite Abbey up above town. building style has changed to more southern stucco and pastels, and North Africans abound. so beautiful a cloister at the Benedictine Abbey - i'm growing to love cloisters... these loggia-lined and arcaded gardens walled away from the day, places of contemplation and tranquility. each pillar top here is carved with Bible scenes or decorative animal designs, and a towering old Cedar whispers songs the mourning doves refrain.

Bastille Day, 14 juillet and everything is closed but for one boulangerie - making a killing. grabbed two slices of pizza for now and a baguette for tomorrow. crowds gathering for the concert on the plaza.

7/14/2004

early morning light etches
   window panes blue
       in foreign room,
     treetop birdsong fire spreading.
  my sleep-drenched eyes
    brighten,
       another day along the trail,
saffron sunflower sangha bows east.

7/14/2004

crushed white Quercy
    limestone trail,

    some favored fruit in season
making bird-shit blue.

7/14/2004

la jolie belle
    la jolie belle
        la jolie belle chaleur...

waited whole fucking Cambridge
    winter windchill long to be
    sweating like a Sunday whore with
        Monday bills to pay.

wild grass gone to weathered grey-blond seed
    feathers the narrow trail
        through valleys shimmering with
        yolk-gold sunflower blooms,
    vertiginous as staring into stars.
        and something has
            changed ~
the hum of the heat in the vineyards,
    black plums hang ready to be teethed,
        wild fig trees by trailside,
            Moissac's
            pastel stucco facades,
    and men of Algerian shades ~
walking walking walking...
            suddenly as a spell cast
                i've entered le Midi.

44 | James Timberlake

7/14/2004

Moissac abbey cloister ~
    ancient cedar limbs sweep sky
        raining grace and
            quietude
    upon reflections of the day...

walking due south,
        morning sun licking left ear
            deeply...
      first the Scent,
    then two blue-clad peasants emerge
goat bleat chicken squall sun
      from shadowy barn depths,
    each a white crêpe paper rustling mound
        of crated Garlic in his arms.

friends along the way
    exchange addresses, parting here
      in cedar shade.

journal - 7/15/04

spent a few quiet moments in the morning church before heading
into the hills - leaving Moissac, still moche, ramshackle, rundown.
steep ups and downs, vineyards, plum orchards, the guy with no
pack - no nothing - who passed me yesterday on the sycamore
road passed me again this morning. that's traveling light. aspersed
by a quick-pivot irrigation gun, the trail wended the valley for a
while before giving into Malause - views of the Tarn and Garonne
plains broken by regimented poplar plantations. 'great' view of the
nuclear power plant towers surrounded by sunflower fields. long
stretch across scorching corn plains to Espalais.

peaceful vine-shrouded patio and grassy green backyard at the gîte in Auvillar. it's well below the town. looking forward to a crudité tonight as the body is craving raw vegetables. will see what the Petit Casino has to offer. the 'Transbaggers' i passed earlier by the canal have arrived at the gîte. happy loudness. festivity for its own sake. they're all mid to late 50's, at least a dozen of them. some walking, some driving luggage, some taking turns.

7/15/2004

belch
    reflux
        remembering ~
in sphere one-thousand-year-old
        eyes,
    walking stick
          raised against
        Greek sea blue skies
            to hook and gently
    bend wild
      plum
            branch
        down
to sun-chapped pilgrim's lips.
    sun-warm
        sweet fruit flesh.
    a few breaths grin around the chewing,
      a moment never ends.

journal - 7/16/04

last night in Auvillar, oooo la laaa Georges and i joined Michel (French) and Elisabeth (Québecoise) - two pilgrims on the trail who've met and mated - for apéritifs. they're staying in a private gîte up in the village proper. decided to put what we had together

46 | James Timberlake

and eat out on our leafy back terrace - crudité, moussaka, pasta, wine. Georges has travelled to the Himalayas, throughout India, Peru - had the chance to buy a hand-rubbed sanskrit 'Life of the Buddha' and 'Thol Bardol' in Nepal but it was too heavy to pack. bumped into him in a Saint-Antoine café this morning.

walking tar lanes through sweltering sunflower and hay fields - a painful heat-rashed day. 33K? and up to Flamarens, up to the soothing church in Miradoux - my body steaming cauldronly in the cool temple shadows.

end of a hard-broiled day, Lectoure in the distance, walking towards, the town never seemed to get closer. steep ascent. friendliest "bonjour!" from an old guy in a white wagon strengthened my steps... but the gîte is full! crap. an additional 25 minute walk down to a hotel the Office de Tourisme directed me to - and who's there but the 12 Transbaggers! the herd from Normandy, le Troupeau Normand who applauded my entrance! eyes hot with emotion. perhaps i'll never see them again but this amity in foreign lands is eternal.

everything outside has gone russet pink... sunset effect on a stone hilltop town.

7/16/2004

finger-long lizards scuttle
        in/out
    deep fissures in the sun-crackt clay trail.

Saint-Antoine,
        church and town samely named ~
    seems some sainted hermit had his arm
            from elbow severed,
                dipped in reliquary silver and
                    jewelcase displayed
                behind a chapel's glass wall.

        in this place and time
                all sunflower fields erupt with
                        yolken blooms,
                all hayfields mown
                        and mounded
                                dry.

7/16/2004

long
                        long   hot
                sweat-drenched
ascent through
                        woof and weave
                sunflower fields
                        to Flamarens.

behind July-tempered
                copse leaf shield...
        resonant Babel.
                Original Birdsong
                        echoes in
                                black shade.

7/16/2004

this cricketed hill
        overlooking ruined castle walls,
                pilgrim's lunch in oaken shade ~
who bore your forebear's acorns
        watched arms and banners change.
                tomato sausage cheese and bread i
imagine taste much the same,
        but to you is bequeathed the crumbling,

48 | James Timberlake

the crumbling of an age ~
one white cloud hovers now
   in baby lite blue sky,
      the vapor from reactor stacks
        so close to idyll's lie.

7/16/2004

brow, forearms, thighs
   roasted brown,
     walking
through buzzcut
     hayfields,
     heat leaping back to sky
         writhes
     the horizon-reaching
sunflower fields van goghsian.

Miradoux église,
   body steams in cool stone temple air.
      outside, swallows squeal
      and shadow-flash
   the blue draped queen of heaven,
     red roses at her feet,
and i'm a-calico in stained glass window light.

7/16/2004

Castet-Arrouy church.
   thick piled Romanesque stone sanctuary
      and porch of wood
        inviting sit and shelter
   among close copse shading trees,
      and tout le gang
   is here...

Ste. Bernadette kneeling before a blue and white Marie,
        "viens-à-moi" etched below
            her Son's sandaled feet.
    Carmelite cream and mantled brown
    Ste. Thérèse de l'enfant Jésus.
            Ste. Jeanne d'Arc in leg armor.
    the shepherdess Ste. Germaine,
    innocent roses tumbling from her apron,
    a hand on the head of her loving lamb.
                and tonsured St. Francis
                coddling his dove...

from when and how they left France
        and arrived in Québec who knows?
who knows when and how they made their way
        to Maine farms and
            1930's 40's 50's churning Androscoggin mills
    and now back to peasant hamlet France
                in my bone-born blood.
                    there is
                archetypal comfort in
                        these incense
                        wisping walls.

7/16/2004

sun-cracked lips and
        wind-parched throat,
    battering heat from sky and tar,
            soles burn,
            right knee grinds,
                eyes squint from bright shimmering hay,
    the shaded hilltop respite
        still so far away.

laying naked on hotel bed...
    showered 'til the soap
        was gone
    and used up all the towels.

journal - 7/17/04

for blisters, rash and general pain i'll spend two nights in Lectoure. slept not well at the hotel - no air circulation, woke to thunderstorms that only added to the humidity. sent more stuff home, more crap i'm not using, scales of the dragon falling away.

the woman at the Office de Tourisme let me in the gîte early and i went out in search for grub for tonight and tomorrow. a crudité is in order - it's what i crave in the heat, and it is HOT. emailed everyone - oddly i had only a few paragraphs to say. hard to concentrate with the Tour de France blasting decibel 10 above the bar behind me.

got an email from Nate. the fat nasty bitch-ass cat he's had since college died and he wants to collect peoples' memories of him and put them together into a tribute. the cat spent a week alone in the Boston College dorms with a broken leg while everyone was away on break and i think that was when he went mad. fucking thing used to attack my ponytail from behind when i was sitting on the couch. found this gothic 'poememory' of him trampling me after one of the summer Pig Roast Bacchanals we used to have up on Academy Hill in Brighton.

7/17/2004 - Jerry

pork-meat belly bloated,
    drunk and stoned and sprawled
        upon Gem Ave's latenight August lawn ~
  one among a 'nam of Pig Roast fallen brothers.

through a fang slashed tear in space / time
and honeysuckle hedgerows
he barrels otherworldly thundering...
Jimmy, BelaLugosi-bolts upright rigid and wide-eyed,
counts froze-breath seconds
before his onrusht doom...

flame maned, talons forged by Vulcan!
Hell's Juggernaut Cat bashes me back to sprawl
and upon my flesh-rent chest
shrieks infernal harpy howls
with bitter enmity for every blessing bestowed on Man.
then,
Jerry vanishes into misty
blue lit dawn.

bar le bastion
lectoure, france 17/7/04

7/18/2004

grey cropped
hay hill field,
milky sky,
lone crest tree swallows crow with a cry.

7/18/2004

humid heavy skies,
mad Pentecostal wren
magic-fluting field from overhead ~
sun-cracked clay trail
strewn with i-ching
straw fallen from a random
tractor bale ~

such Sunday silence.
     wondering what trod thee scarab
          and thee toad
               to death upon a country road.

7/18/2004

sun burns
     cloud and fog
          away,
     longest morning shadow
          draws me
               westward
          to the sea.

journal - 7/19/04

yesterday, left Lectoure under heavy skies after breakfasting with the quiet Basquaise, and two Bellicose Belgians who stayed at the private gîte in Auvillar with Michel and Elisabeth. apparently they love each other but quarrel frequently and didn't much walk together. the BBs smeared their thickened stew from last night on toast... onion, lentils, miso, pumpkin, parsley. she loves Annie Proulx and the Brontë sisters. he was quiet and expressed himself with a dry reserved sarcasm. they both had the drawn faces of the Macrobiotic.

alone most of the morning. followed the Basquaise for a while. she walked nicely, planting soft steps. a short Suisse dynamo named Clara passed me, but she was going only to le Romieu today and soon stopped to enjoy the tranquil countryside.

played the waiting game with another pivoting irrigation watergun drenching the field. at one point the trail passed through a strangely sunflowered junk and tire dump that's a Ginsberg or Kerouac poem. met Didier resting at the Ste. Germaine Chapel - he's afflicted with foot pain. walked with him slowly. i found it tiring not to keep my own pace. Catrine joined us on the way into Condom - classic view of the church-crowned town from a distance.

disappointing meal - prawns were good, duck breast was shoe leather. the cavelike pizzeria that i had gone to years before and anticipated for weeks was closed on Sundays.

Didier's phone alarm went off unintentionally at 5:am and the room began to bustle. followed the river for a while - more vineyards, but still the predominant fields of sunflowers. took the variante to check out Larressingle - a windowbox flowered and hollyhocked 'bastide' - a community where church, château and stone homes form the surrounding rampart walls. nice, but it has that faux facelifted feel.

Montréal-du-Gers. like Auvillar the entire town-square's fringe is a loggia - to protect from heat and weather, i imagine. crumblingly enchanting cheap hotel, hot dusty attic to hang wet clothes in. thunderstorms passed over. le Troupeau Normand! and they invited me to dine with them tonight.

strange strong neon floodlight in the center ceiling of the church, another Romanesque old beast.

short étape to Éauze tomorrow.

7/19/2004

pheromone-ecstasy yellow butterflies
   rise double helix dances
      in hayfield updrafts.
   trail turns.   breeze freshens.
     horse hooves pull ears, then eyes
       to classic age-old tiers -
low clustered peasant hovels,
   hill-crowned castle keep,
     faint sun in milky sky.

suddenly, one howling black dog attacks
    suddenly, one spotted hound whips hedge round,
        me thinking
      'shit i'm gettin' double teamed!'
suddenly a comic book tackle dust cloud rolling,
      Spot chomps Blacky
        by the nape
    and rump-humps him into submission's silence.

channelling mad mountain hermit laughter
        shakes corn rows,
    yellow scented
      corn pollen
        settles,
the sound of stars.

7/19/2004

nearly blinded by
    sunflower-stoned
      kamikaze butterflies,
i sit field edge
    for pilgrim's lunch ~
      a smile remembering fat old woman
      walking in Lectoure,
    jowls, belly, tats and thighs,
      each jiggling its
        own rhythm ~
irrigation watergun
    bursts volleys
      in the corn,
    my eyes
      searching for a privy tree.

journal - 7/20/04

enjoyed eating with the Troupeau last night. hell of a storm outside tossing the treetops. after everyone left lately, (waiting for the storm to lessen), the Matron let the dogs out and they had a friendly fight on the diningroom floor. she showed us pictures of how one of the dogs came to her - shot twice in the neck. now he never leaves her side. the other scraggly dog had three legs. birdcages stacked like crates outside riot in the wind.

uneventful walk through Armagnac vineyards following the long former rail track to Éauze. beautiful in a lush way, but monotone. walked into Éauze and got the last bed in the gîte. at the café with Didier, Catrine, and Jean-Michel - who is a bit obsessive and manic - never stops fidgeting. he once snowshoed across the Aubrac! this barman is a riot - deadpan, droll, one speed, a 'pince-sans-rire' they're calling him. wants to massage all the ladies' shoulders and turns his back to anyone flagging him down.

7/20/2004

    bar terrace chair,
        eyes following silhouette swallows
        through day's end sky,
    cloud-berg noses
          peach sunset beams,
      dives baleinic into
        the night.

journal - 7/21/04

the whole gîte, plus le Troupeau Normand, packed the terrace tables at Bar la Commande last night - M. Laberthe, (the old droll troll), treated us to some kind of Armagnac cocktail.

56 | James Timberlake

up and out by 6:15. morning vineyards... grapevine trimming tractor like a great Praying Mantis hacking its way through the rows. maybe for the addition of topsoil and manure over the years, but many trails today through field, vineyard and pasture were deeply set into the earth. made it to Manicet in good time and had a hot chocolate. decided soon thereafter to skip Nogaro for countryside peace and made my way further on to Lanne-Soubiran. hot, humid... less and less of fields and more widespread forests.

passed an older French couple on the way to L-S. they're staying there too. the gîte is a converted barn with thick, brightly painted beams. sat long in the grass watching a slow storm approach over the valley, thunderheads entrancingly lit from within, and practiced doing nothing at all.

'sad' story about how my sneakers followed me by way of Jean-Michel. they're too heavy to pack any longer and i left them under the bed in Éauze. J-M saw them, kindly took them, carried them all day, and since i didn't stay in Nogaro he handed them off like a relay baton to Arie the Dutch pastor - oops. in typical Protestant fashion - jokingly, but typical - he said i should have to carry them the rest of the way for penance.

7/21/2004

leaving Éauze...
thick tropic air holds
a floral honey scent,
acrid brush smoke
veins pulse the early
morning air.

for last night's brief rain,
forest respires
valley haze into
boulder rolling thunderheads.

7/21/2004

through fern
      forest growth...
  carpet, drape, and valence
     ivy vines...
light blue sky laced
      canopy leaves...
    trail winds to open sun-touched visions.

over mown hayfield stubble
     one wide of wing hollow-boned
        falcon flashes penetrant
        reptilian eyes.
  tufted milkweed seed and horizon collide.

between meadow and pond
    a spiritually bull-balled prawn
      raises claws to take on a
         heavy-booted pilgrim thinking
how i had your cousins in alfredo sauce with tagliatelle,
     and step quietly
       aside.

the dense wind
    baritones by ears,
rhythmic walking ever on

through as far as the eye can see cornfields'
    flapping green leaves,
      nature's watery applause.

7/21/2004

Lanne-Soubiran's calm hillcrest,
   white plastic chair in
      perfect pose ~

i watch towering
   thunderheads on the slow approach
      glean deep energy from
   verdant wood and vineyards ~
long crisp lightning sparks fissuring,
   amorphic sheets flashing blue-rose within,
      60's Star Trek bell jar
         throbs an all-powerful Mind.

journal - 7/22/04

last night was my first time at a Chambre d'Hôte - odd to be at a stranger's kitchen table, but pleasant. Bernard and Annie were the other guests staying in the actual house. we chowed down a baking dish of cubed potatoes topped with confit duck legs - roasted until crispy - the spuds absorbing the delicious duck fat... a tin of fleur de sel on the table.

left the sneakers behind at the gîte again and after about a half hour the Chambre d'Hôte lady chases me down in her car to return them! nooooo! Pastor, la Suisse, and B & A all had a good laugh.

walked with B & A all the way to Aire-sur-l'Adour. B liked to point out and name the flora. he also liked checking where he was according to maps and GPS and photographing signposts of the towns we crossed. had an Orangina with them in Barcelonne-du-Gers and the bartender brought over the livre d'or - the Register so many bars and cafés have for those passing through to write a note in.

lying in bed i heard le Troupeau Normand pass below my window - almost shouted down, (Aire being their last stop this year), but rather just enjoyed hearing their familiar laughing voices echoing along the road and fading around a corner.

7/22/2004

the silence man's
    steps bring
        to bright summer field ~
    boiled-egg cheese bread
        apple tomato prune make
            here a quiet pilgrim meal ~
branch-clung cicadas cadence
    crickets in the hay ~
lacing these weathered leather boots,
    i wonder if they'll make it
        over the Pyrénées
            and across the long heat of Spain.

7/22/2004

first morning light,
    gently closing dormitory door behind me
        FOG
            transfigures distance into
            billowy blue-grey shades,
        invisible Gregorian turtledoves intoning...
forest, fern and flesh along the trail
            rhythmically dripping dew,
        wild green walnut fruit tumbles,
    one slug,
        one stone,
            one dead bloated shrew.

Aire-sur-l'Adour's Cathédrale St. Jean Baptiste,
    XIIth Century silent piled stone ~
      entering into cool gloom
    3-o'clock half ton bells thunder deep foundations.
a whisper from Jesus written on an altar card,
    "venez à l'écart et reposez-vous un peu..."
"step away from the crowd and rest yourself for a few..."
and through scratchety speakers
    YoYoMa's cello stringing Bach crescendos.

    the skin electric tingles,
      tears trailing
        through my beard.

journal - 7/23/04

proudly leaving Aire-sur-l'Adour at 6:20 - screwed up reading a balise after the Stadium and followed waymarkers through a creepy forest - paused at the glimpse of a deer - attacked by a Taon Swarm - and found myself back in Aire at 7:30. shit.

not long before Miramont-Sensacq i felt like not wanting to go all the way to Arzacq-Arrazinguet. with the additional 7K, that would make a 37-38K day - not doing it. Miramont is on a calm hilltop surrounded by plains - would be a view if not for the haze. met Jean-Michel by the church and found he made the same unintentional detour! earlier by the pond i came across a gimpy Québecois trying to push his overladen bike up a steep hill - very heavily accented, very animated, "un p'tit shove s'il te plaît!" J-M thought he was crazy.

warm Acceuil at the gîte offering freely coffee, juice, beer, cold water. three women operating the place - seems like overkill.

maybe they work at the connecting Mairie? will eat with them tonight.

Marie-Pierre, Pascale, Jeanne - they belong to the Friends of St. Jacques Landaise and do a weeklong tour of duty at the gîte - welcoming pilgrims, cleaning, cooking. a farmer - the GR65 goes through his land and he stopped by to chat and see what it's all about - he stayed for supper - thick accent - red shirt - one brow. i was man of few words - quick conversations and i need more time to form phrases.

7/23/2004

hazy
    hot and
        humid
hours through corn plains.
somewhere they're spraying
    pig-shit in a field ~
        detour to
            Latrille,
        no café.   nothing.
    there goes that
        morning-long
    hot chocolate
        dream.

7/23/2004

cornfields   cornfields
     cornfields   cornfields
cornfields   wild fennel cluster spices breeze
          cornfields   copse
               cornfields   cornfields
copse copse   cornfields
     cornfields   copse
pine tree plantation   cornfields
               cornfields   cornfields
                    powerlines
cornfields   cornfields   cornfields
     cornfields   copse
     cornfields   poplar tree plantation
          musky stream   copse
cornfields   cornfields
          cornfields
               cornfields
               cornfields
     men wrapped in plastic
          pulls and aprons crackle
               sysiphusly snapping
          cornstalk tassels
               down the rows of
cornfields   cornfields
          cornfields   copse
               cross a busy road
                    cornfields   cornfields
     copse   cornfields.

journal - 7/24/04

slept well - woke early - left by 6:00. the bustling Centre d' Acceuil in Arzacq-Arrazinguet is like a cluster of college dorms - must be a hub for vacationers.

nearly crushed a bird underfoot entering the church. sitting... breathing... falling over to the left.

Lionel and Olivier are here, as well as an Opinionated Blond Frenchman from Perpignan proclaiming the superiority of his language, and that on principle he would rather starve than eat before 8:pm. i asked him how he liked his principles cooked and went back to my meal.

7/24/2004

    opening early morning
        gîte door   rooster crows

wondering, 'should i worry?'
   black rabbit scares across my path
      beneath momentary
   evening star morning star
         Red Sea upon Pharaoh's men
     horizon clouds descend and
        engulf me
     boot-crackling a stoney trail,
        breathing rain washed wafts of hay.

crossing the threshold to Wang Wei's silk screen dream,
     fog phantoms even the brow-near
       branch,
  peacock's strident gobble
      shivers valley haze,
   spiderwebs
      capture spheric moons of dew.

journal - 7/25/04

Manic-Old-Guy loves walking fast and marking time. this morning his timer beeped at 6:am - packed it up quick and bolted out the door. he's in my room here in Arthez-de-Béarn. morning stage was the nicest of the day. high hills and deep valleys, back to cows, many dogs. at least they're chained and gated - except for the two at the XIIth Century Chapelle St. Pierre who never let me close enough to visit.

good meal down the road - as everything is closed up a normally closed up too restaurant owned by a local made everyone at the gîte a simple 10E prix-fixe meal of wine, fish soup, grated carrot salad, pasta, porc cordon bleu, and an apple-filled fritter.

7/25/2004

a pause,
    and a poem written ~
        grasped walking stick
           slick
    with mountain fog
        ball and sockets
            smoothly in the fist,
      metronomes
        the day.

7/25/2004

after fruit
and tea,
walking into the dark morning
sweet with hay.
out of fog
the pond appears,
misty blue trees
along the further shore ~
one trout
chirrups.
meniscus ripples
back to still,
and boots grind rhythmically
carrying on.

7/25/2004

bright hot noon,
belly full of lunch,
grassy trail
serpentines
corn rows.
manna millionly
wild white
morning glories
bloom upon the ground.

7/25/2004

between July high cornstalks and
     fern-berm walls
  the daylong trail winds through
      Louvigny,
    Fichous-Riumayou,
       Larreule,
Uzan,
    Géus-d'Arzacq,
        Pomps,
    Castillon ~
all agricultural, i.e. not a
  goddamn café or bar
    hamlets.
burned nose
  stone bench
    oak shade,
wind from west freshens
  hazy sky to eye blue.

journal - 7/26/04

Manic-Old-Guy left early. fog cauldrons among morning hills. met up with the Doc at the grocery in Maslacq - no bread delivery on Mondays. spoke with the friendly grocer - old woman waiting behind me shuffles her feet attention-gettingly, but he kept on talking.

Sauvelade. the owners here have got it made. find a place on the trail where there's nothing between étapes but an attractive ancient church and a couple ruins and open a pizza / sandwich bar with a small gîte. when i arrived, Maurice - the mad biker with swollen knees using his stripped down pedal-less bike as a mule - he was here gnawing on a sandwich. i appreciated the calm and decided to stay.

Clara, again with Bruno, stayed as well. i made crudité, she made
a tortilla de patatas, he ordered pizza from next door. gentle
conversations - Bruno is an ice cream artisan in Germany and
spoke of the experience he had years ago - of crossing the Pyrénées
at night by the light of the full moon!

7/26/2004

Arthez-de-Béarne,
   hilltop hamlet -
      yesterday's refuge from
      lashing sun.
        a shower
          a meal
  a bed -
now, dawn's
   rose wisp hieroglyphs whorl
      world-old silent chants -
shins damp with dew
    i descend again into
      lowland cauldron
        fog.

7/26/2004

    dark and silent temple
  stone surrounds...
     against the bright blue stained-glass Madonna
        wrapped in rose
        and golds
   a doomed fly hyphenates
zzzzzzzzzzticzzzzzzzzzzticzztic
zzzzzticzzzzzzzzzzzzzzzzzzzz
zzzzzzzzzticticzzzzzzzzzzzztic.

7/26/2004

leaving Maslacq,
    poplars massaging early morning fog
        echo Pau River water rippling
            root and wind and leaves...
    even that cloud up there delphic-dizzy
        with
        corn pollen musk.

journal - 7/27/04

early morning walk on narrow lanes - followed high hilltops mostly. a few pasture deer.

met Maurice in Navarrenx - he was chomping rare bloody steak between his rubbery lips for lunch wanting to fortify before the 'nothing' to - in - around - and after - Aroue. says he's biked all around Newfoundland, Alaska, Central America. funny guy - clownish expression like a man with his false teeth out... like that French actor / clown in 'Delicatessen.' Manuel is here also and is always talking kilometers.

Mireille at the barbershop trimmed my beard. the grooming by a woman's hands felt so good.

7/27/2004

dark threshold stumble-dance,
        feather clatter and coo
            turtledove takes flight from eaves
    into south clouding north clears
        sky,
        Venus
        pierces.

observer mind molts
  under Milky Way eyes.

    for one moment
  th'eruptive sun burns
      all
    into
        essential silhouette.

      or
    four snort-laughing hogs
  gambol glee in morning field
until one hits the electric fence and shrieks ~
      all freak,
      mad scatter,
      gone.

journal - 7/29/04

left Navarrenx yesterday about 6:00. on the hilly trail Manuel
came up behind me... slowed down pace and speech. wants to
do the trail with a donkey - his brother has one. mutual Bush
Bashing. palombiers in the trees - dove hunters' elaborate high-
limbed blinds - tension between them and the ecologists every
September. when he was crossing the Pyrénées a few years ago in
a sea of clouds he heard Basque shepherds singing back and forth
across a gorge.

we must have been slowly climbing - as the fog cleared, deep
valleys appear around the trail. more sheep and goats than cows
now. long hot walk up to a mountainside chapel surrounded,
Stonehenge-like, by sycamores entwining limbs. across the valley
- the Pyrénées in all their different shades of blue. met an old
guy up by the panoramic panel that indicates the names of the

70 | James Timberlake

distant mountain peaks. he loves history and maps - understood him perfectly as he went into great detail about the Cathedral of Burgos, of the synthesis of Northern European and North African arches that came together in the Cathedral of León. later at a ruined church he pointed out the reception room that welcomed medieval pilgrims making their way through bandits, wolves and wilderness. arrived in Ostabat about 17:30 - beat.

the farmer who ran the ramshackle gîte brought us homebrewed Muscat in a wicker-wrapped plastic jug and we toasted our apéritifs. ate with the Family, the Bald Man, and the Cooking Student who mentioned it is now forbidden in France to make 'fond de sauce' in restaurants! they have to buy it pasteurized!

had breakfast with the Family, (French Dad, Mom from Oporto, two beautiful brown children). on the way to the fields the farmer dropped off fresh eggs, which Mom boiled. leaving the gîte i ran into Maurice! he and a trail friend didn't get in to Ostabat until after 10:00 last night. just missed him. we left about 10:30 from the bar. 'we' being Manuel and the three hilarious storytelling Belgian cyclists. won't ever forget the fat mustachioed barman's Ricard-effusive grin.

overcast morning, lush high hills, heavy mist. Basque white / red painted villages are striking among all this greenery. grey clouds wrapping mountains making most invisible. walking through the rain... man chases a stray cow back to the herd - chatted for a moment - jocund - all smiles - wife works in a chocolate shop in town. will drop in to see her tomorrow.

throngs of people in the Saint-Jean-Pied-de-Port medieval quarter... shops, restaurants, pilgrim info kiosks. i'm eager to find a cheap hotel.

7/29/2004

cool morning,
    quiet trail,
        sky swells
            with eastern light ~
trees hide horizon-rising Pyrénées.

cock crow
    churchbell
        dogs bark
            woodsmoke swirl,
out of one eternal
        moment,
    the wide world falls
        into
            place.

7/29/2004

head down,
    mist gathers,
        hat brim dripping rhythms,
            steady footsteps along a trail ~
white walls,
    blood-red shutters
            latched tight
            against raw day...
Basque farmhouses manifest out of the fog ~
        the scent of someone duck-fat
            frying onions
makes a bone-damp pilgrim
    pause in reverie.

7/29/2004

white fog blanket,
   dog's
                   bays
       float
one
   sheep
     bell
       across
         invisible
           mountainside.

7/29/2004

between cowbells
     clanging hillsides,
  church tower rings the hour ~
haybales sweetly
    fermenting
      massage my mind.

fog veins stream down valleysides.

     mists,
       then rain ~
   the white silk billow sky
     descends to suckle
       mountain heights,
     descends to lowland whispering brush
        wanting
      to listen to the earth...

  a couple comes up
    behind me singing
      in a foreign tongue.

journal - 7/30/04

saw Maurice and his trail friend who i'm now realizing looks like Dr. Zachary Smith.

wonderful woman at the chocolate shop - she laughed to tears when i said i met her husband on the trail. said he's invited pilgrims to their home many times - once she came home to 22 people tenting in the backyard! 'Have you ever made coffee for 22 people!?!'

lunch - brandade stuffed roasted red peppers, roasted duck breast and frites dressed with red pepper cream.

skies slowly clearing. pale moon is full. i wonder...?...

7/30/2004

6:am wren song
   splashes misty meadow.
now,
    too deep an afternoon
      sun massage
      rubbers my bones, water bottle
         so
           light ~
at silent hamlet's edge...
B scrawled,
     A,   a crooked R
  on broken
    tree-nailed board
      windlessly phantom rocking.
  table and three chairs dark with shade...
hesitant   wondering   parch thirst,
    abandoned? but someone waters
      the potted geraniums ~
    cupping eyes to window
    stubbed hat-brim rattles glass ~

dog barks crash
        off cool stone floor.
                i walk away.
            key tapping pane calls
                me back...
"oui?"
fading red-rinsed hair,
        ruddy cheeks
            a little vacant behind the eyes...
'i wanted to make a restaurant of it
        but my husband died.'
her Basque brother -
        a shepherd in Utah,
                worked like a fool,
        he bought a home here in the mountains,
                heart attacked and died too.

she took my empty beer
        bottle,
                flung it in the ditch then hobbled
            to smallness at the end of the road
                to put a scrap of paper
                        in the bin
            with the same sense life makes.

crossing ancient Roman
                footbridge,
head back, drinking deeply,
            the bottle she refilled wet
                    with condensation...
sweat crimps eye,
        white egret
                circles and
                        sails over the near horizon's
                                hill.

Upon This Stoney Holy Year | 75

7/30/2004

Cathedral meditations -
   coked-up croupier card
     scattered mind
       blaming footsteps,
         voices,
       back pain for distraction
  belies...
     belies...
cloud front belies mountain
  mountain belies cloud
    map belies clouded mountain
  clouded mountain the map belies
     and laughing inside,
    Christ walks upon the storm.

journal - 7/31/04

woke at 1:am, packed, and walked down a silent rue de la Citadelle - the stone pillars of the Porte d'Espagne were studded with tiny lights - then the gentle climb began. humid, mild, peaceful under the full moon with the mountain shadows i'll to be walking into yawning high ahead. ah, to walk at night! crickets, dark homes, trepidation's thrill through black tree tunnels. up, up into the jagged shadow-cut mountains, Saint-Jean-Pied-de-Port growing smaller and dimmer behind.

walking meditation following the full moon winding through mountaintops... experiencing a deep peace i hope to be able to always tap into. bright Venus behind, the sinking moon ahead growing in size, going pearl, amber, peach, then sanguine at the horizon. daylight spreads, powerful rushing winds begin. ate an apple overlooking the east-reaching range's shifting shades of pale blue, molten sun, eagles soar.

steep beech grove shelter and the rinsing sound of leaves. Fontaine de Roland. the stele marking the entry into Navarra - first walkers coming the other way - "Buenos Dias!" and i walked steeply down to Roncesvalles about 10:am. fatigue behind the eyes. the Abbey's reception isn't until 3:00. and since there's nothing in Roncesvalles but the hotel, the Abbey, and memories of Roland i decided to continue on.

took the first hostal in Burguete and it's dear. foreign language tension from expressing myself well in France to now's fragmented words, seeing the strain in the other person's eyes crackling crows feet trying to understand me. chucked the first pair of socks - growing holes. fucking flies.

8/1/2004

2:am. Saint-Jean-Pied-de-Port.
   bootsteps echo cobblestones
      over the river Nive to la Porte d'Espagne
        shimmering with embedded lights,
  and i walk away toward black mountains
     cut against the field of stars.
       moonlight takes over
         where streetlights soon end.

through time... shepherds singing herd-song vale to vale,
   cutthroat bandits on pilgrim's tail,
      a peddler's cartwheels tramping sheep-shit,
  Charlemagne's men, Ganelon's betrayal,
      Roland falls,
     a song arises.
Napoleon and me through the Pyrénées
    winding well beyond
      the sound of steeple bells.

well beyond the sound of steeple bells sheep snore.
    the invisible thunder of wild horse hooves.
        bristle-mane hound growls blackly.
          so alone, terror crawls skin.
    a trembling flashlight beam beamed in his eyes...
        growl becomes anguished yowl and he flees.

now upon a stone outcrop made just for this...
    to stand toes clasped to the precipice,
        two legs walking-staff and mind
          over cavernous gorge,
    full Basque moon blooms
        convolute currents in clouds low below,
          the silken light fading in deep ravines.

stopping to piss and stretch spirit arms
    from west-setting bloodred moon
        to eastern predawn stars,
          hot wind from Spain blows against my face,
French mountainsides steam, vanishing behind,
        new country days ahead.

8/1/2004

after all night walking
    through Pyrénées
        peyotic visions and
          skin-eroding winds,
    deep eye dawn fatigue ~
hunkered in mountain beech grove shelter,
        napping beneath
      rinse rustling leaves...
    this soft disintegration
        in flickering blue light.

journal - 8/2/04

in bed in Burguete... early morning i began to hear the ceaseless tapping of hikers passing by the hostal - walking sticks and footsteps tapping tapping tapping... spirit sinks. how many can there be?! poking my head out the front door looking left and right - herds to either side.

with the sun still behind the mountains, i walked out beneath flashing rose colored clouds - through tight Basque towns... up into low mountains - the musk of boxwood permeating.

in Larrasoaña - a long line of bedraggled sun-whipped peregrinos at the albergue - whistled 'walk on by...' and did.

followed a river thick with trees, could hear picnickers below splash, fish, and barbecue. towering storm clouds threatening all afternoon were held at bay by mountain peaks - a nearly visible energetic claw holding back the front.

long hot urban walk through Villava and Pamplona suburbs - the refuse strewn Magdalena quarter - Cathedral rising in the distance - quiet Pamplona streets. 5:30. 39K. damn sore. called Josefina's nephew Guillermo and settled into her apartment on C/ Nueva.

8/2/2004

still in bed.
    Burguete morning.
        below my roadside window
        what the hell's that
        metallic tapping...
                thought dawns...
                shit.
            pilgrim throngs
                leaving Roncesvalles ~

out the front door i could have been in a mall.
   spirit aches.
      bike tires crush by,
   encroaching footfalls.

mountain pass.
   sun smoulders
      delphic boxwood ~
      only an opiate,
   the day's deadly mind remains.

journal - 8/3/04

morning mercado - fruit, almond crunchies, chocolate dipped palmeras.

visited the Cathedral and its high-arched cloister. i want a cloister.

threatening storm clouds finally erupt during postcard writing time, umbrellas fly and crash on Plaza del Castillo - dust devils arise, kids scream.

lunch with Guillermo in the ornate Café Iruña and laughed about the vote in Roncesvalles - not really a town but they vote like one. the same results every year - the 18 votes from the priests and religious always on the right, and 6 votes for the communist party from those who work in the two hotels. then to an extensive Henri Cartier-Bresson photo exhibit in the Citadella... black and white frozen motion.

journal - 8/04/04

left late - 9:00. Perdón mountains always ahead. through blond-cropped fields, similar towns dotting the plains - square steepled belltower and stone church surrounded by white stucco-walled homes. reticence arising, the garbage scattered outskirts of Puente

80 | James Timberlake

la Reina - first albergue is full - second is ramshackle surrounded by tilled dirty grounds, crowded dorm.

it's work for the spirit and mind, but it is interesting to focus on awareness regardless the conditions. watching mind. tilting left meditation in Puente's Church of the Crucifixion with a Y-nailed Christ and another Madonna holding orb and Child.

8/4/2004

    leaving Pamplona's hearth healed and rested ~
ancient trail current sweeping
  body/mind westward,
    August ripe sunflower heads
      shedding petals, bow.
  morning clouds mirror
    mountains in form and shade,
      mist freshens.
every other footstep rhythms
  10 o'clock
    steeple bells.

8/4/2004

Puente la Reina ~
  the baroque belltower's
  gold lichens against Navarran blue skies,
    white stork imperials over
      roofs from his
        shag stick
        throne.
  walking broad day's
    dark narrow streets,
      scent of dog-shit
      ribbons hot wind.

journal - 8/5/04

not the nicest trail today. it followed just off the main road, which was itself under long-distanced construction. stunning approach to Cirauqui whitely capping a mount. had pastry with sticky raisins there, and a beer later in Lorca. met up with Bruno! thought he would be well ahead of me by now - was thinking yesterday of emailing Lionel to get B's address and thank him for planting the idea of crossing the Pyrénées by moonlight, and then he appears!

Estella. Iglesia San Pedro de la Rúa piled atop a stone outcropping - closed. Iglesia San Miguel - closed. Iglesia San Juan - closed. commiserated with a Spanish couple about how all the churches are locked up all the time and they agreed. also commiserated about how everything is dirty - trash at the entrances and exits to the towns. and all over the steps leading up to San Miguel - disintegrating plastic bottles, papers, broken glass.

city-wide fiesta tonight - dance music in front of Iglesia San Juan, throngs packing the plaza, smells of churros frying, roasted pecans and cotton candy spinning. a lot of crap to buy - bobbles, trinkets, handbags, black black Africans selling pirated CDs and DVDs on bedsheets. kids on mechanical broncos, kids flying through the trampoline room, kids on the plaza kicking a soccer ball, which landed in a pram - got yelled at... landed at an old crone's feet - got yelled at. the sights, sounds, faces and emotions of the Fair.

8/5/2004

mountains crossed,
   another foreign land.
      glaze in the other's eyes
         trying to understand
         my stumbling tongue -
last night rainclouds broke open.
      now sunbeams sweep the trailsides,
   mown hay stubble crackling
         dries.

journal - 8/6/04

woke early and out by 5:00 - crappy cement neighborhoods - glad it was dark. quite a few walkers but nothing like the crowds leaving Burguete and Pamplona. climbed, then skirted the mountain behind Estella on a tightly treed trail, a couple palmfuls of wine at the Monasterio de Irache's wine fountain. landscapes of distant cliffs, sweeping plains, lavender fields and vineyards, green olive groves over red tilled earth. the new trail family is emerging familiar and kind.

decided to stay in Los Arcos and not carry on further. sweet woman working at the albergue desk - gaining confidence with my Spanish. a new refugio - smaller rooms. that first night in Puente la Reina was overwhelming - 50 bunks in a cavernous old hall.

8/6/2004

standing in morning hazed
    purple mounded rows,
  sweet pine penetrant
    lavender scent
      steeps mind.
forearm and leg hair quiver
  with bees' wing-wind and
    yesterday's Polish boddhisattva's words,
  "I am really happy
  to be here."

sweaty hard night's rest.
  slept just deep enough to
  skirt dream and wake to
    some drunken cow snoring
      between rough sheets in
  bunkbed cluttered hall.

trying to pig-wallow thrive in
      fatigue,
all this garbage strewn,
    road construction,
      factories,
        insecticide,
'better off elsewhere' blows on mind's malign coals.

high trail,
    sweaty chill ~
  palm still smells of 6:am
      wine pouring out
    la fuente d'Irache ~
    just this,
  moon-white cliffs dawn rose
    and a lavender-field sieved wind ~
Polish boddhisattva's words ring bells,
    "I am really happy
      to be here."

8/6/2004

between forest green slopes,
  mown flaxen hay stubble
    bowls
  blue morning skies ~
by clusters
  and alone,
    distance-shrunk
      pilgrims
        saunter into
  vanish.

8/6/2004

from my boot-toe proceeds
    the long white and
        winding trail ~
mown hayfield's flaxen stubble sprawls across
        tilled plum-red earth,
    slate mountain cliffs rise
        into the blue
            where jet contrails
        fade quickest from memory.

journal - 8/7/04

woke when the German girls got up and left town by 5:am. wide tractor trail across the plains - olive groves and vineyard patches growing in freeform sprays, not trimmed into hedgerows like in France. coming storm clouds coursing against the wind. lightning and thunder threatening. stopped in Sansol for hot chocolate and cake - cozy café hovel nooked and crannied with Santiago memorabilia.

dropped the Lomo hard on the sidewalk in Viana - eeeeeee. that camera is already on borrowed time - light sensor that was kind of iffy last week seemed to heal on its own. on borrowed time as well with the boots - they're starting to crack.

Zorongo concert - medieval, flamenco, moorish - supposed to take place in the ruined roofless Cathedral next to the albergue. would have been cool but the storms dictated a change of venue.

8/7/2004

strange western stormfront
    barrels on against the wind.

moon and
    dawn part
        my shadow

        color-relief-detail
            returns
out   of   blue   silhouette

        silvery olive tree leaves
            shimmer
        over the golden Spanish
            land.

8/7/2004

brush tucked
    and unzipping...
        thought to millennial
    pilgrims' piss shit spit and rag along the way.
        wood chips and chicken bone shards
            sold as relics to
        those sauntering
            westward.

arms on café bar,
    spoon spinning hot chocolate
        in heavy bottomed glass.
i fondle
    polished key chain
        bobble,
    walking staff and gourd
        burned into the grain.

journal - 8/8/04

last night i made a ratatouille with garbanzos, fried a couple sardines, cooked an omelet and ate with the French women. glad we made too much... fed Oliver and the two Italianos who arrived after the grocery had closed. all three passed me on bikes today shouting their thanks.

5:30am. dark walk winding the edge of town, then out into the plains - nearing Logroño i froze, breath stopped - the largest meteor i've ever seen! a pale green-blue-white fireball streaking across the sky.

descent into Logroño - nondescript sprawling modern Sunday morning city - everything closed - no one around. left through new parklands - young staked trees - empty garbage cans and trash all around the benches. came across Zoli by the manmade lake. Hungarian. back of the knee tendon pain. gave him a handful of Aleve and we walked on. didn't stop talking but he was pleasant - tales of India and Thailand...

passed a immense bull silhouette statue that i think was in 'Jamón Jamón' - stopped at the café by the refugio in Navarrete, waiting for the 1:30 reception. broke down little city. tomorrow's etapa - a long 36K.

people were bemoaning the lack of food. i checked the cupboard and made 'Indian' lentils - clove, garlic, peppercorn, cumin... ate with the French ladies and Mariko from Japan.

8/8/2004

before dog herald dawn,
　　a pilgrim again into night,
　　　　half-moon light softly glows
　　　　the cricket chirped meadow and trail ~
　　　　　　walnut-wide pupils
　　　　play grapevine
　　Rorschach shadow games ~
now'n again
　　　　near birds napping
　　flare feather song at my approaching footsteps ~

breathing deep to it all,
　　strange coming clouds
　　　　blow against the wind,
　　silent flash lightning sheets...
'red clouds at morning,'
　　walking staff mast wavers.

8/8/2004

　　leaving Viana
　　　　early morn,
last night's music
　　　　still rings marrow...
　　medieval instrumental phrases round
Gypsy and Moor diphthonged cadences
　　like stream-stones that whorl the current
　　　　swaying head and shoulders,
　　　　　　hands to heaven rise ~

now, clouds flit a half moon,
    ring around a Venus,
        boot crushes snail shell...
trail too dimly lit to find
        and finish off a suffering.

wind marionetting
        knees along
and dancing tree-limbs' shadows,
scattered crickets chirrrrrrrrrrup
    fields,
            nearing Logroño
flesh halts.
        breath stops.
            jaw drops.
        eyes fan wide to meteor streaking
blue-white flame reddish and green four full seconds
    across a new found frictive sky.

8/8/2004

café afternoon,
    Zoltan's heavy Hungarian accent intones,
        "Hey, two flies just fucked
            on my t-shirt
            shoulder."
    table bursts out laughter to the skies.

journal - 8/9/04

churchbell chimed for the first time at 4:am. leaving Navarrete -
dark walk into the grapevines - rain begins and lasts. it's warm.
rich green colors over red earth. low dark clouds swooping the

hills - Alto de San Anton. industrial entry to Nájera - hot chocolate in a bar watching weather gust by the church's massive columned steeple. continued up into the pine forested hills, which opened out to broad plains of rust-red earth, dull hay, and distant villages capped with church and steeple.

Cirueña. storks in the church tower. petting a scrawny pale blue-eyed cat i slipped on a mossy stone, and flapping arms in backpack imbalance, tumbled over. if i'd have seen me i'd have laughed. caña con limón at the bar - guy assiduously scrubbing the fountain outside.

Santo Domingo de la Calzada. found a cheap room above a dive-bar restaurant - 15E. those miraculous chickens that Alain and Jacques told me about back in Conques are in the church here - at the telling of the story this place seemed so far away.

8/9/2004

crickets burrowed,
    eave-tucked birds,
        leaving Navarrete in dark early
           morning, rain crackles
hat brim, trickles shoulderblades,
electric amber glow over distant town
    burning prehistoric time...
        i, my last meal.

rain intenses draining clouds.
    from an Alto de San Anton
        cowl-dry tree copse...
light lime and dark green vineyard leaves patter shadows
        against coppery tilled earth,
      blue silhouette mountains
        appear.

8/9/2004

between Azofra and Cirueña,
    eating crusty-loaf folded cheese
  on the shorn hay plain ~
      small bright spot growing larger, brighter,
becomes a cyclist, left arm waving,
    Babel Hungarian/German/Czech/Russian
        part speech, part song, part wide white smile...
    and in Pentecostal mind i hear-glean
'all the world's a temple.'
    small bright spot fades,
      black clouds thundering.

8/9/2004

walking walking daylong walking
    under spent thunder skies.
azure mountain jaws gape
    la Rioja's golden plain.
blue panted men bag snails in
    tall trailside grass.
ants fester round providential boot
    crushed slug feast.
a tire flattened sundried frog-chip
    tosses me an
        injun 'how.'

journal - 8/10/04

left the restaurant last night, followed the sound of music and was ushered to a seat on the spacious plaza to watch the Play! 'los Milagros de Santo Domingo.' awesome al fresco show - the life of Domingo - a Xth Century hermit. he wanted to establish a hospital to help pilgrims through the deep woods here, offering them protection from Bandits and Wolves - hard to imagine now.

he succeeded despite ridicule from locals. a lot of political stuff i couldn't understand. the play included medieval dances, juggling, fire eaters, a cavalry that shat all over the cobblestones, pyrotechnics, death of Domingo, release of a dove and the reenactment of Santo Domingo's miracle. it was great! "Santo Domingo de la Calzada - donde cantó la gallina después de asada."

slept well and late. visited the Cathedral, the shrine / tomb of Santo Domingo, cluttered with side chapels and bye-altars. the statue of Santa Generation - St. Anne holding Mary holding Jesus - Anne and Jesus holding an illiterate medieval symbol - the sphere of perfection in their open palms. Convento San Francisco covered with stork nests. looking up at one point - must have been 20 storks gliding the sky pterodactylly.

after last night's play an affection is growing for the hermit Domingo Garcia who was so moved to help pilgrims on the way he pounded a roadway, (calzada), a bridge, a church, and a hospital out of the wilderness. bought a few of his trinkets, a meditation chaplet with shells for beads and the cross of Navarra.

tonight - back at los Caballeros - more blood sausage stuffed with rice, bacalao and wine.

8/10/2004

cutlery
    clicking cheese
        course plate ~
    wine bottle dregs
        freckle a crystal glass ~
ancient satisfaction giving way to ancient ache,
    long leg muscles long
        to carry spirit
    further on down
            the westward
                trail.

journal - 8/11/04

left about 5:30 into dark plains. several shooting stars, slow and steeply rolling hills. Grañón - quiet streets, magma clouded dawn expands over the church square rustling with trees. chocolate pastry in Castildelgado. Viloria de Rioja, two friendly dogs nipping. walked with Jerome whose friend's 17-year-old daughter committed suicide - he's walking seeking answers. deep blue skies, cool wind blowing all day in the face. made it to Belorado early. happy to see Isabelle in the grocery.

the crumbling town's sycamore-lined square with a bandstand in the center. lot of walkers pit-stopping for a few hours before carrying on.

closely packed bunkbed dorm room. i have an upper bed in front of the windows in this rickety old building attached to the church - ruined castle walls up the hill behind.

ate with Jerome and Mariko. i made a crudité with garlicky vinaigrette. Mariko made okonomiyaki... seafood, green peppers, eggs, flour - like a pancake topped with a mix of mayo and soy sauce. Jerome made pasta with tuna and tomato. beers with Robert from Alabama - been teaching English in Madrid for the past five months - he's walking with Iana, a German woman. enjoyed speaking English smoothly! at the bar a rocking old lady card game was going on.

8/11/2004

damned delicious latenight coffee's
   toss, turn, and sweat.
   i finger maestro
      churchbell tempos
         through the wee ~
Navarra. la Rioja. now the Castilla y León region unfolds.
   Santo Domingo de la Calzada diminishes behind.
      ahead, falling star
   dark plains brighten blondly
      below dawn's cloud wisps...
chest thumping winds never ceasing.

tick infested mad-dog mind
   snaps at air and visions,
      bleeds by its own claws.

on the heights, Belorado castle ruins
   are nothing now ~ mortar clumped stone,
      but
on the heights, hummock throned,
   daylong wind rocks me
      harping pine and hay,
   blows to bone this face away,
      sweet cleansing.

journal - 8/12/04

was woken at midnight by local fuck-wad bastards yelling
"FUEGO!" ... 'Fire!' and chucking water balloons through the
open window - everyone got soaked.

up at 4:30 and out by 5:00. hard morning. muscles aching in the

94 | James Timberlake

cold winds. faint moon soon clouded, rolling hills, a few partially ruined / deserted villages. walked with a woman from Biarritz who stayed in Tosantos with Isabelle and Martine - two other French women i've paced for a while. walked long in pleasant silence with her.

after climbing up into the Montes de Oca, trail evened out and wound through oak and pine. nothing in San Juan de Ortega but the monastery. continued on, hoping that the upcoming albergue in Atapuerca isn't full up. only 20 beds.

got bussed away to the archeological site and it wasn't that interesting. the tour was all in Spanish, which isn't a criticism. but it was all lecture. no bones, no tools, no nothing but looking at rock and saying here is where these artifacts were found. me and the other foreigners kind of shrugged at each other at the site.

8/12/2004

latenight
     fuck shit local
   rat bastard youth
       yelling "Fuego!"
waterballoon volleys burst against
   once cricket peaceful open window
     walls,
 soaking all.

leaving early,
   silver sliver silent moon
      and Venus soon clouded.
        particular dark.
        grateful for a smooth trail ~

west-born raw sea and sky winds
       gel marrow,
    muscles squeal over bone.
        walking on,
   morning sun barely warms calves.
      long shadow whispering
          ego pride and ego pity
  fearing cold cudgeling gales in the heights
      but finding oak, pine, and purple heather
          shelter there
     from siren shipwreck songs.

journal - 8/13/04

woke late, left late, and walked with Robert and Iana a while - she
was teaching him a German children's song about three little pigs
sitting by a river, one puts in a foot, one a snout, one a tail.

through dry plains, a couple villages, then in Villafría the nastiness
of Burgos began... miles of industrial miasma, hot tar and oil, car
factories, machine parts, semis, concrete drum-mixers roaring...
but actually the change to 'thriving urbania' charged me and made
me smile as i proceeded longly to the center, grime collecting on
the brow.

striking Cathedral facade against a bright blue sky. inside - kind
of cold, a marble museum, no spiritual resonance. went to the
concert at San Pedro de la Fuente. more music from Alfonso X - 'el
Sabio!' will look him up at home.

journal - 8/14/04

slept deeply at the hotel in Burgos. strange dreams of powerful
Spielbergian clouds and tornadoes.

96 | James Timberlake

Burgos museum - paleolithic scraps. all the diggings from Yacamiento Atapuerca. UNESCO declared it a world heritage site because of the new 'Man' found there that paralleled the oldest remains found in Africa. i should look up 'desposorios místicos de Santa Catalina.' no idea what that means. i've seen another representation of the story somewhere before but i don't know the background. Santa Catalina surrounded by cherubs, and i think she's being given a ring. another Santa Generation, but this time with St. Anne holding a flower instead of a sphere. mainly religious art. Roman relics. dolmens down a corridor leading to a burial circle.

i should look into a writer named Zafón, too - his <u>Shadow of the Wind</u> is in all the bookstore windows and everyone is reading it.

journal - 8/15/04

walked out of Burgos - peaceful moments through a poplar forest - a rave going on in a corrugated garage - then the gunshots started. dogs bay and men in the distance with knots of birds strung at their hips. passing through Tardajos, through the remnants of an all-night town party... drunken bedraggled tattooed youth, semi-trailer trucks in a row packing up equipment, smell of Ducados and Kalimotxo.

the Meseta! an expanse of 950-meter-high plains. all one sees off to either side of the crushed stone trail is nonstop shorn hay, on and on and on. Hontanas, 0.5K away - looking around - nothing in sight. on and on and on. several of us looking at our guidebooks and shrugging. a valley dips in the Meseta and there it hunkers. a simple stone hamlet and junkyard, hasn't changed in 500 years. smell of sheep on the wind. this area has its own particular beauty, which may turn to madness by day six, but for now it is engaging. what a shift from urban Burgos!

Upon This Stoney Holy Year | 97

8/15/2004

    leaving Burgos...
moonless bright stars,
    black rustling poplar
        plantation rows and open plains ~

    behind a XIIth Century country chapel,
    6:am corrugated metal barn seams strobe
    thumping teen rave techno ecstasy
        laughter and screams ~

        bird-hunt's first day,
            gunshots echo ripples
in the mist ~

Tardajos village fiesta remnants,
        slick black van swallows the band,
           bedraggled blear-eyed youth
           haunt park benches, bullfight
posters plaster walls,
Ducados waft, (el sabor latino, i.e. burning trash),
    piss and Kalimotxo ~
        sniffling the dripping,
    taste of lake water lapping in my nose.

8/15/2004

hot Meseta wind
    crusts sweat,
        evaporates mind ~

crushed stone
        piles wake
    red clay trail
        through shorn
           wheatstalk plains
    to blue horizon line ~

the only shadow
    glides away
        below dragonfly wings.

journal - 8/16/04

after the menú last night of fried pork slices, two fried eggs, salad, and watery garlic soup - up in the square anchored between the church, the restaurant and the gîte, about nine guys, glassy eyed with beer, start balancing tree trunks upright against each other in teepee-style and packing the inner space with hay. at midnight they torched the pyre, it lit the night and the mood was surprisingly calm with about 50 people hanging out watching the fire - then, when it collapsed crashing in sparks and flames the music and dancing began! how many centuries has that been going on?

up late, up early, warm morning, bright stars. stood among the ruined convent of San Anton's pigeon cooed echos. stopped in Castrojeriz for a hot chocolate with the crew. steep ascent into high flatlands. stopped in Itero de la Vega for snacks - chill kitten there, resting on my belly.

i'm finding the Meseta meditative - wind in the ears constantly, the enchanting subtle beauty of bright wide plains rolling. followed the Canal de Castilla to Frómista - Martine and Isabelle, and Mariko!

8/16/2004

leaving Hontanas' village cluster,
    last night's bonfire crystaline coals
        glow thousandly spark-eyed
            when the wind blows ‑

feeling the echo... Big Bang flung constellations and
   stellar mist, brilliant behind
      rippling clouds ~

stopping to piss,
    feather and birdsong burst from the brush,
      time shifts.
     one stone glows with starlight,
   ruined pillars appear in the dawn,
      footsteps press blessings
        against my earth.

8/16/2004

over cobble walled-up portal,
    carved saints and Bible scenes erode ~
where Antonins once
    layed Tau to fevered brow and
      played therapeutic flutes before the lepered,
       the gangrened, the pestilenced,
   the spirit-weary seeking saintly healing
    in this mellow clime.

standing among
    the San Anton convent's
      crumbling walls,
   i tilt head back to collapsed-open skies,
    so sweetly deep in
      coo hoot pigeon echoes...
    crisp feather wingbeats
      tapping.

journal - 8/17/04

from the Frómista albergue i stepped out into coldness. that, plus a body that walked 38K yesterday - a lot of pain. turned into deserted Población - eerily lit 'Salem's Lot church up on the heights, daylight growing, threatening clouds. turned into Villarmentero de Campos for a sign indicating 'organic bread' - agricultural hamlet, a few turns and a modest outdoor bar opened up - green lawn, white chairs, hot chocolate and croissant, boombox basso Gregorian chants intoning through the grey morning. the barista tosses old bread to strolling fowl. took the variante through fields and away from the road. several wrong turns. rain begins and slowly thickens, thinking – slow to start, slow to end.

Mariko showed up at the Carrión de los Condes albergue. she's loving the bottle of wine that comes with the menú peregrino and was very talkative.

8/17/2004

sun lashes calves –
      i watch long self-shadow
    recoil beneath my feet
        and listen to Alpha-Omega-less mind.

8/17/2004

from anemone wave
    wisp clouds to
        thunderhead-anvil ringed fields,
    i watch my daylong shadow
        dial round to cower beneath these noon feet,
and for 20 paces
    western sea musk scent entrances.
      on thermal uplifts, eagle
        corkscrews to invisible heights.

8/17/2004

early morning pass
    through Villovieco -
silver-blue dawn light briefly sweeps sky.
advancing black stormfront prow
    fills eyes,
        squeegees raw wind
   across Meseta plains
     into   every
        single
        puckered
        pore.

journal - 8/18/04

left Carrión - not early - avoiding the cold, finding the rain. hat-brim and head down low watching the trail. i was soaked but not cold until the last few K. so much for the warnings for this etapa about the lashing heat and bringing enough water. got to the albergue and i was the first to enter, everyone else was at the bar waiting.

at the bar now - three cafés con leche and three whiskeys - it's packed with people wrapped in ponchos and plastic bags ducking out of the storm for a fortifying dram before continuing on. like in a New England snowstorm - one mind - everyone having the same experience, everyone smiling against the common atmospheric enemy.

Brazilian guy working at the albergue was constantly mopping up the floor after dripping peregrinos passed through. genial sign in the dorm - only one i've ever seen as the albergues normally get everyone out by 8:am so they can clean... "A good night's sleep is a treasure. Sleep well and get up when you want."

twiddling time on my poncho draped bunk, waiting for 8:pm to eat.

wine, soup, rabbit, tart, and patxaran.

8/18/2004 albergue meditation

breath ~
   breath ~
      plastic bag crackles under
         searching fingers ~
  ass-gas thunder baritones
        a seated toilet bowl ~
      breath ~
        breath ~
          breath ~
     bathroom door latch snaps ~
       sandy sandaled footsteps on
         wooden stair ~
clothes dryer tumbles
     zipper clatter ~
  clothes dryer tumbles
      zipper clatter ~
breath ~
   breath ~
     Spanish conversation, vale! vale! ~
      CD flute warbles ~
     bunkbed springs squeak ~
venga! joder! vale! ~
     breath ~
  wooden prayer beads
     softly clicking ~
pilgrim priest's robes rustle by ~
  backpack zipper scree ~
   wonder what i did
     with my underwear?
      breath ~
   breath ~
    velcro sandal ripping.

journal - 8/19-20/04

yesterday. cold. bright rainbows connecting disparate stormfronts after dawn as i entered Ledigos. walked with the German girls for a while and had hot chocolate with them in San Nicolás del Camino. Sahagún albergue is in a former church nave with carrelled bunkbeds. made lentils on the two-burner stove and ate with Isabelle and Martine - Mariko made carbonara in a bag.

several times as an early morning wake-up call a soft flute played the haunting X-Files theme.

today was cool, but ever so gradually warmer. no one on the Roman Road.

stopped in Calzada del Coto for a cheese sandwich and CCL. picnic tables in the lady's kitchen where she cooks for people walking by. Isabelle and Martine there just before me having breakfast. mountains come into view. ran into a small group of bohemians in a field - Pole, French, Spaniard, Austrian. they spent the night under the stars fishing for little fish.

found the albergue in Mansilla de las Mulas and ate sardines and pasta with Père Eric walking in a long black cassock. the patio - bright with geraniums. plenty of hot water to wash clothes. none for the shower. guy at the grocery saying pilgrims are down 70% - last year at this time there was a line of backpacks down the road. i showed up at 5:00 and had no problem getting a bed. seems they were overzealous warning people about the crowds during this Holy Year and everyone stayed away!

first i hear of a Holy Year. when St. James' feast day - July 25th - falls on a Sunday that year is designated as a 'Holy Year' and anyone making this pilgrimage within said 'year' gets their Sinner's Sheet wiped clean. bully for me!

classical music concert at the church - i.e. cultural center - that

upset Father Eric. he refused to attend. 'sacrilegious to use a church
like that.' the capitalized Church doesn't seem to mind.

8/19/2004

rippling magma dawn sky ~
   far rainfall blurs
      western horizon, there, there,
        and there
  that two rainbows bind.
    cold winds with no promise
     of warming blow ~
fist stiffens to the walking stick knob.

8/19/2004

strangers, handshakes, names, cigarets,
   sudden kindred spirits in
     stream-rippling field.
philosophical conversation's pause,
     something deeper blows.
   three faces turn westward,
    listen the wind
      in their ears.

8/19/2004

my horizon stretched
   dawn shadow long ~
     sun rises, nothing warms
      the day.

big black spot
   in flick'ring flock,
     wrens chase crow away.

8/19/2004

left right rabid self-
    lashing mind,
        birdsong unbinds.
rustling poplar copse upon
           wide Meseta plains,
    demons and swine.

8/20/2004

    cloud-shade and sun
        glide
           caresses
    over wind-purred plains ~
        temple crow's feet
    tighten
        and
           ease
the muscled mind ~
scattered distant
    rainfalls, pillar-anvil
      coming clouds,
        almighty sky ~

    skin quivers
      with one smile,
        steep blue
           mountains
  rise.

journal - 8/21/04

slept so well on the upper bunk. left about 7:30 after a dog kiss. mellow walking. from behind me the dog-kiss dog comes frolicking an hour later. it belongs to Miguel. good English. lived in León for a year working in the penicillin factory. "I love León!" he repeats over and over. showed me the tradition the bars have of giving a tapa freely with every drink ordered.

meditation in San Isidoro. coffee and pistachio ice cream here at the Ékole Café - Armando y el Espresso de Bohemia CD playing. coffee tweeking. got to walk soon or burst.

met up with the Brit from Viana who took my advice and mailed back a bunch of crap she wasn't using, but clinging to all the same. walking much easier now. found a neighborhood bar and enjoyed chorizo al vino - sautée garlic and onion, add chorizo to brown, and deglaze with enough red wine to stew... bread to dunk. "I love León."

journal - 8/22/04

watched some latenight TV. X-Files in Spanish, CNN in English, world news - Bangladesh bombs, Al Sadr is still in his mosque, US election quibbles. Flamencos - musicians and dancers - Manolete, Tomatito y Michel Cometo, Manolo Sanlucar. from 5 to 8:am when bars and clubs shut down there was a constant stream of loud drunk humans down my road.

strolled the river to plaza San Marco. awesome bazaar... olives, candy, socks, sweats, kid's clothes, shoes, sandals, fabrics, handbags, plants, nuts, sunglasses, costume jewelry, CDs, bras, bikinis, nylons. i bought a leather change-pouch and a cool Arabic scripted coin to twiddle.

8/22/2004

León.
    stroll weary,
        i settle spine deep
            against cool Cathedral stone,
    absolutely erased in
        stained glass
            kaleidoscopaphasia.

organ thunder, organ rain,
    organ boulder landslides,
            time-lapse organ garden sprouts,
        blooms, vines twine pillars,
            canopy sky,
    organ ocean seethes the shore,
        organ reikis mind.

eyes open,
    empty silent stone.
        sculpt Cathedral door cracked open
            to the night.

journal - 8/23/04

long walk through the outskirts of León. coffee and tortilla in a
neighborhood bar with a fish in a vase. in Chozas de Abajo an old
guy wheeling a wheelbarrow told me i was going the wrong way
and set me in the right direction. didn't feel like doing the whole
etapa and pulled into Villar de Mazariffe - dry, bright and dusty.
Albergue Tío Pepe - stucco-walled patio harboring an old lady
coffee klatch. i'm fatigued.

many people passing on through to Hospital de Órbigo. French

108 | James Timberlake

pod i saw saying the rosary on the trail had lunch in the crumbling church's shade. blue sky all day. pretty over these sandy ochre walls.

family run albergue, festive feel at dinnertime. potato, carrot, red pepper, pea, tuna, tomato, onion, egg and bean salad with a dollop of mayo in the middle and a tortilla wedge on the side. Daughter - waitress, Mom - cooking, nine-year-old Son behind the bar, Dad - strolls.

8/23/2004

belly blessed with
    Barrio de Pinilla bar's
        café con leche and tortilla bocadillo,
    their flower-vased goldfish ogles me
            from among the dusty bottle rows.

Chozas de Abajo hamlet -
    sun, rain, and time swole
        August apple tree
    ground-bows branches down.

8/23/2004

before heat and sweat
    lube backpack shoulder
        straps...
    squeaking   creaking
            strongly walking westward sways ~
    saintemarièmèrededieupriez
    pournouspauvrespécheursmaintenant
    età l'heuredenotremortamen
            hums ahead.

Upon This Stoney Holy Year | 109

me fingering
    one found red stone
        and metta phrases.
   footsteps,
      breath,
         pores,
  the Camino sings.
      pale half-moon through
        the royalest blue sky,
hot wind carries all away.

journal - 8/24/04

left Mazariffe yesterday fairly early - hot chocolate and toast in a Hospital de Órbigo bar - guy playing slots with barking dog sounds. old woman in the church greeting pilgrims, offering the sello. landscape changing dramatically as the Meseta bumps up against Galicia - irrigation channels flow through corn and vegetable fields, rolling hills, and oak forests.

Astorga albergue, shaded courtyard, water and vinegar fountain for to soak the feet, gentle hospitalero, incense, airy music. it's peaceful here, i'll spend another day. Mariko! made dinner for her - pasta with Roquefort and chorizo... lentils with tomato, red pepper, onion and fried garlic.

went to the fair and bought a Chinese pendant Mariko said meant 'dragon.' lot of North Africans and Peruvians selling trinkets at the bazaar. they must follow the fiestas. went on an awesome ride. "I want go I want go I want go,' says Mariko... ok, fine. El Pulpo! 'the Octopus' whipping round, fore and back and bouncing up and down... 'I WANT STOOOP I WANT STOOOOOOOOP!!!!' screams Mariko. i laughed my ass off.

8/24/2004

trail pebble meditation,
    grasshopper snaps left
        and all creation crashes
    purple heather puzzle piecing yellow hay
        in green oak shade –
        nearing blue mountains hide
            the sea.

journal - 8/25/04

morning stroll - crunchy almond pastry. made an omelet with the leftover lentils.

Alice and Patricia - Irish hospitaleras spending time at Rabanal and Astorga. sat there long yammering away with them. what a hoot listening to Spanish with a brogue. it's Javier's birthday and the wine was flowing as well as the jamón, salchichas, tortillas and empanadas. people just coming by for a stamp are invited in for meat and drink with general generosity. Javier said his wife is pregnant and he wants her to give birth today, but she's not due until 9/5. wants to go home and scare her. his Father owns the Gaudi Hotel around the corner. set up this San Javier albergue for his son to run and maybe make a living on.

Gaudi museum is more interesting as a structure - more Madonna and Child sculptures, ornate silver crosses with impressed Bible scenes, Santa Agueda statuettes with her lopped-off breasts on a platter, Roman steles, ancient money, some modern painting.

homey bar down a side alley - prosciutto legs hanging behind the counter in different stages of slice away. hearty happy barman really wanted me to try their special beef stew. i didn't agree with Father Eric 'that the trek across Spain is more spiritual,' wanting not to practice a division in spirituality, but there is a sense of hospitality here that is actively supportive for those on the trail.

journal - 8/26/04

slept well except for the mad snoring Italiano who'd snore flat on his face even. up at 6:00, out by 7:00. said goodbye to Javier and wished him luck. trail was divided into quarters by Murias de Rechivaldo, Santa Catalina de Somoza and El Ganso. had a hot chocolate and french toast tapas in Murias - old man and wife turned extra home space into a cafe/bar - talked about the unusual cold and the lack of pilgrims this year.

got to Rabanal early - a mellow hillside community refurbed anew. newly carved trail on the way into town through oak woods and upon soft earth instead of hard-packed rock and clay. the Brits don't open their albergue until 2:30.

church doors are open but inner gates are locked against the gold. i am tired... travel weary?

journal - 8/27/04

not travel weary. poisoned! waiting for the refugio to open yesterday - headache - stomachache - burning chills - went directly to bed and they let me sleep in all day today. Patricia is here and has been kind. she put me in a secluded room and maternally checked in on me several times. maybe i had bad water from a well? maybe i caught a microbe?

recovering. napped, strolled - quieter crowd here now than on Thursday. Martine arrived! she and Isabelle split because Martine was walking so slow. something's up with her ankle tendons. and Isabelle had to arrive in Santiago by a certain date in order to return to work on time. older French guy - much interesting historical knowledge but mouthy about showing Islam force.

8/27/2004

long dawn shadow,
        cold flesh,
            hot chocolate
tweaks sphincter...
        eyeing a crumble stonewall ~

hoarse blowhole sounding turtledove
        Gregorians
            mountains
                from blue
    to rose.

8/27/2004

coccyx handclasp,
        cobblestoned hill-town stroll.
            from windward to lee
                a breeze in the trees
            changes tune.

8/27/2004

where the village ends,
        unpressed cement pebble crumble
            seams road to earthen track ~
crickets, flies, recycling bins,
            "tu papel es importante."
watching dust devils tasmanian down tomorrow's trail,
        blue mountains are still
            whether suns
                rise or fall.

8/27/2004

shallowest gravel niche
     in sunbaked stonewall.
pink hollyhock blooms
     nod in eternal August breeze.

journal - 8/28/04

heard every hour chime but somehow still rested well - up at 6:00.
drank my hot chocolate in the foyer and thanked Patricia for her
kindness. walked out with Martine. mountain trail flanked with
purple heather. blue mountains off to the left.

Foncebadón - completely crumbled hamlet. the Iron Cross piled
high with stones people have carried to place here. rustic isn't the
word - a prehistoric albergue in Manjarín. walked with Barcelona
Victor of the mud-stained white pants.

El Acebo - stoney mountain outpost with iron and limb braced
balconies i wouldn't stand long on. small grocery - yogurt and
apple and energy bars - guy from Prague, the Frenchman, (showing
Islam force), and his meek and mousey wife - 'not a racist,' he
repeats, 'but.' he noticed the roof shingles here are similar in
Lozère, and the use of solid pre-Roman cartwheels.

Molinaseca - queer elderly grocery man with cataracted eyes. he
told me to watch out for the women in Galicia then tried to grab
my crotch. i found another grocery.

8/28/2004

purple tufted heather
        froths round
    mountain oak and pine in
            rose dawn light ~
        there when the bones
    brittle, when
                the flesh
        dries.

journal - 8/29/04

quiet Sunday morning. left Molinaseca in the dark. urban vegetable garden clutter and wrack entry into Ponferrada - must have been an impressive city with the Templar Castle on the cliffs overlooking the river, mountains behind - the mountains i followed all day yesterday coming abruptly down to these plains.

walked out of Ponferrada through suburban semi-industrial neighborhoods. engaged by a ruined brick factory, looked like a Fall River mill scene. Taberna Mateo - crimped beer bottle cap fly-guard doorway strings pulled aside. warm smiling patrona, she brought out the pilgrim book for me to sign and the sello if i wanted a stamp - asked me to remember her in Santiago.

walked alone for a while through more roadside agriculture, roadside church with an old man attendant. most churches, if they're open, have a greeter taking down your name and where you're from. this is the first who asked where i was born.

it's getting hot and i'm basking in it.

from behind me comes Matej - Slovenian - young idealist, international relations - a student wanting to be a peaceful politician turning the world's forces from greed and power. long talks about meditation and language. walked straight through Cacabelos, my intended stay, and met up with some friends of his... Laura - Irish, two Brasileiras, and two Italianas. Laura spent time in Berkeley selling ice cream. she loved telling the kids about Leprechauns, "O sure, I've got two in me back garden, like. They keep poppin' the clothes off the line!"

they stopped for a shade break. i moved on to Villafranca del Bierzo - passed the Municipal and went to the private refugio, a creaky timbered, dark welcoming mountain nest.

descent into town. broad plaza. three churches. San Francisco - ornately inlaid and painted wood ceiling. San Nicolás - interesting that the retablo was mainly dark wood and not rubbed gold leaf. the 'non-racist' French guy is here. he noted that the Spanish often put a windowed cupola over the altar for illumination. the Basilica - unadorned. four massive internal pillars with the domes above entirely studded with bare round stones. stark beauty.

8/29/2004

leaving Molinaseca,
     early blue morning light,
   insyncopant rooster eruptions
       through Bierzo Valley plains,
    footsteps to silent adoration.

8/29/2004

walking stick swings
    between thumb and fore,
  the metal tip ticking pebbled trail, cobblestone,
     smooth cement, curbstone, ribbed culvert, tar,
flagstone sand, aluminum can,
    sewer drain and hubcap...

i stop by a rambling roadside
   rosemary bush with German woman smiling
      to break off aromatic sprigs
        for backpack strap tuck
   "mmmmm potaytoes bayked with rosemary,"
     she says dream-eyed ~

agricultural hamlets sprawl upon
   the Sunday plains...
of asters, dahlias, cornflowers, mums,

   passionflower flowers, and fruit-pendant limbs...
of plucked Brussels sprout stalks, overgrown fields swollen
   with bright-warted gourds, pumpkins,
     pig-belly melons basking,
       tomatoes aglow on browning vines and
  the fig tree consumes a collapsing shed.
a sundressed woman mops venetian blinds clean,
   blue panted men scythe, claw, uproot,
     and bundle stalks,
       stoke white to black smoke coils.

   to linger at
village bar 'Taberna Mateo'
   for two beers,
     a cheese bocadillo
incensed with thumb-and-fore
   crushed rosemary
     ripens
   my trail soon ending mind.

journal - 8/31/04

two days of great beauty - great energy!

yesterday, followed the winding valley floor through villages that hug the old road - Trabadelo, La Portela de Valcarce, Ambasmestas, Vega de Valcarce... stopped in Vega for a CCL and a few groceries. didn't look like there's opportunity to buy provisions up in La Faba. old guys hawking walking sticks and trinkets by the church in Ruitelán. steep ascent to La Faba.

the albergue is run by a German Confraternity of St. James and is exquisitely organized... all plates - the same design and none of them chipped. Kristof the Quiet German arrived - invited him to lentils - "best he's ever had," he says. lentils La Faba. sautée onions and garlic - later add carrots, water, red wine, dry lentils, diced tomato, diced red pepper, rosemary, tomato purée, adjust seasoning and drizzle with olive oil.

we went up to the bohemian albergue manned by an Israeli crew who spend six months in India accumulating trinkets, then six months here selling them to passers-by. beers with German girl and Kris explaining that a Stuttgart businessman gave 250,000DM for the albergue - anyone from the Stuttgart area who sang one of their regional songs got to stay there for free. he sang and bought a round.

woke late. continued to climb. vibrant morning mountains. feeling so good in O Cebreiro - two CCLs, crunchy almond pastry, affable company passing through. hard to press on enjoying everyone so much. peculiar old guy in... Fonfría? sitting in the shade, he warned me about terrorist bombs in Santiago. bizarre.

stayed in Biduedo wanting one more night in the heights... admiring the Galician mountains behind, the sea of clouds below. Italian guy here, Karín. we managed communication juggling Italian, Spanish, English, French. talk of spirituality is intensifying

118 | James Timberlake

in earnest. he's a gardener. been to South Dakota for a Native
American sundance ceremony. a French Duo pass. similar talk
about the rich living energy in the mountains.

while i'm writing, three times old folks with long canes have
guided cows out to the roll of mountain pastures.

8/30/2004

village to village to village
        through the valley winding,
    dark garage door yawns,
"hola, quieres fruta o fruta seca?" smiles.
        banana in hand, 50 cents lighter and
    thanked simply for stopping.
            sun glides
                the valley's sky-furrow above.
    shy kitten vanishes
        in zinnia
            quiver.

8/30/2004

valley trail winds
    through interlaced mountain talons,
        face wind yin,
    yang sunrise behind,
        a crystal throated river chimes.
            traffic sounds,
    th' EU force-financed autobahn bridge
        rockets
            western mind
            through Celt danced heights ~

chestnut leviathans...
      thinking of those when i
         began this trail in France and in bloom,
   now spiny lime green fruit glow...
     mountain slope balm
       to Meseta-weary eyes.

8/30/2004

lentil stew pot
    shared with German stranger-sponta-spirit-brother
      and beers at
         La Faba hamlet local ~
    leaving...
night dark narrow cobblestreet rich with
     kitchen garden compost musk,
        mountains inked
          against the night ~
between schist church and chestnut rows
    tonight's albergue home
      porch glows,
Santiago's statue,
   staff and
     gourd and
       shell.

8/31/2004

bright full moon,
   light blue sky,
mountain morning shadow
    combs down
      western slopes to
        sip a silver stream ~

trail winds
    cool mountain lee ~
purple heather,
    acrid sheep-shit,
       cock 'n dog duet their echoes.
    before the mind,
bird alit ember mountain-ash berry cluster swings.

8/31/2004

a pause to listen to crickets creaking songs in
       dewy silver broom...
    relaxing a toe the
       spine unbinds.
over updraft coursing mountain heights
    white belly bird of prey reads sinews in the wind,
       tweaks each hollow quill,
    and in seeming motionlessness
       slips across blue skies,
       the vole twitched
         fern slope
   below.

8/31/2004

wind purrs ears,
    sun nuzzles flesh ~
crossing the O Cebreiro pass to overlook
    cloud-tide floods in deep
       Galician vales ~
       crickets, lone green
         peaks,
    this one
adrift under so much blue.

journal - 9/1/04

full moon morning, all the valleys below wallowing in clouds. Triacastela - picked up a loaf of bread dusty with the oven's wood-ash and walked out into the fog i earlier watched seething from above.

Sarria - not so attractive but bustling.

117K remain.

9/1/2004

leaving Biduedo in
    low morning light,
        dark green mountain heights.
   Galicia.   Galicia.
     cool comfort breeze
       and mossy stone trickling
   the night's cloud glean ~
  last time i walked under
      full moon spells
    Pyrénées were my pedestal to the skies...
now, so near journey's end,
     descending into
       milky fog seas
  slowly surging with whale belly cloud rolls,
    i vanish
      into
   the valley below.

9/1/2004

from Galicia's pastured heights to
        old growth valley lowlands,
    schist stonewalls relief
            fern in the mist ~
kitchen garden zinnia's
    red-blotched blooms among
        plucked Brussels sprout stalks.
haybale throned brinded kitten,
    a hunter's eternal whisker twitch.

9/1/2004

night cloud nourished
        green Galician heights,
    blackberries beaded with morning dew
        the lingering moonlight
            pearls.

9/1/2004

mountain descent,
    high valley fog wisps foulard
        brush and tree,
    lowly valley fog thickens
        blending
cows   cars   crows
        train   a truck   a road
            invisible.

white veils
   and sound,
      low thunder...
i hear one thousand wrens
     flutter at my breaking through
         blackberry hedgerows ~
blond banged My Little Pony
   peers o'er the barbed,
     the hay and heather.

9/1/2004

stonewall-lined sunken trail ~
   acorns and chestnuts glow
     the same light green shade
       in white blown skies ~
  fog writhes
     shredding time's Mandelbrot patterns ~
brown corn husks strewn upon
   the sheep-shit ground.

9/1/2004

standing cliffside
   to the knees in green fern ~
deep valley fog blows
     arms, legs, eyes,
      mind, 1,000 years away ~
  stiff beard whisker finds its
   way between lips to tongue
     and is spat
 into
   the milky air.

9/1/2004

daylong roiling brume
   seethes up valley walls.
      just the trail before me,
         a few feet of forest green
        then all is white
     and fog dews the leaves
  leaves   the leaves,
dews beard and brow,
   calm crickets form the invisible field,
      roosted birds,
         the deep wood.

9/1/2004

after Triacastela,
   across a crystal throated
   Celtic brook
      the sun no longer shines ~
forest breathes fog,
   fog breathes cloud,
     cloud breathes eternal mind
       and sylvan green sounds rain ~
breaking through fern and vine tendril,
   chestnut, oak, and elm trunks tremble.
   the white veiled
     green world
       close as night.

journal - 9/2/04

left Sarria early. first warm morning in a long time. followed a
dark quiet trail then hordes appeared out of somewhere. Barcelona

Victor called them 'tourigrinos,' these people doing the last 100K thing and wanting to get to Santiago for the Sunday Mass. i stepped out into a field to let them pass, but they kept on passing!

serious vertigo over the bridge to Portomarín. most 'Massers' stopped there and the albergue was packed. i continued on through pines and fields to Gonzar - a crumbling bit of a hamlet with an albergue and bar. drank bottles of wine with Australian Lance, Emmanuelle, Miriam, Kristof, and Harry - a German artist hiking with his dog. philosophical, spiritual conversations juggling mockery and compassion.

9/2/2004

leaving Sarria,
    dark humid morn,
  mist and shadow braids swarm the trail,
      forgotten old warrior god
       gnarled oak
     suddens blackly,
   draws me near -
     gazing through branch break
      to dew silvered
fields...
   strange,
     warm radiance palpates
      from the god,
    laying left hand upon
  humming bark praying...
   crow fissures cloud,
    corn pollen musks
     the heavy air.

steel walking staffs clacking stone
   spark countless footsteps.
      peregrinos-lite...
         'they-without-white-ankles'
         'they of the last 100K' throng...
  flashlights slash,
      headlamps club,
hola hola hola buenos días hola hola buenas
buenos días holabuenasholaholaholabuenashola...
      feeling i've been struck
        by a Spanish locomotive.

journal - 9/3/04

another misty mysterious morning. heather and yellow flowers
among the foggy pines. crumbling stone hamlets - old folks driving
bovines, cow-shit pattied flagstone streets, geraniumed balconies.
most peregrinos stayed in Palas so the afternoon walk was solo -
nice, but damaged by the heat rash.

walked into the Melide albergue and Ya-el from Day 1 in Burguete,
(and later in Santo Domingo and Carrión), is here. i was making
lentils for tonight and invited her. Kristof showed up with potatoes
he dug with an old man in a field, which i added. Katerina showed
up and i added her carrots. Miriam showed up and i added her
mint... and we all ate together round a table round.

the hot water here is in the kitchen - it got lost on the way to the
showers.

9/3/2004

Galician morning fog
   wraps mountain, blankets away sun,
      sweeps sheets shapes and phantoms
         before my eyes ~
the ever invisible cricket
   sounds an undulant field,
      the deeper dragoned sea beyond.
heather and yellow blooms
   echo footsteps, ego
      fangs mind.
         only 80K until
the incensor swings Cathedral nave sweet.
apple tree blotches
   yellow
      and unleaves.

journal - 9/4/04

slept restfully and late, 7:30. still dark. glad someone clicked on the overhead neons. a woman who i spoke with in Ponferrada and run into many times since was sick and heading for the bus. said she saw Mariko who made herself dinner and drank a bottle of wine, which surprised her. Mariko saying, "Wine very cheap in Spain. I want move!"

beginning to walk through eucalyptus groves. a soft, natural Vicks-y aroma i feel in my throat.

Arzúa - modern, shops, tenement buildings down the main drag, a line of backpacks in front of the albergue, Harry's pack guarded by Harry's dog. will try to find some heavy duty tape for the boots as the inner lining is tearing to rags. earlier i met a husband and wife in wheelchairs asking for money to make it to Santiago. Ya-el saw them too and had the same experience as i afterwards - wondering if they were shysters. but in talking with them the feeling of great honesty and effort arose. we both gave them money - if they're shysters that's their deal.

a stone and thick-beamed albergue - gruff hospitalera wouldn't let the red-haired German biker stay - pissed! guess there's a pecking order of who is allowed in the albergues. only for pilgrims for starters, walkers have priority, those on bike aren't permitted until after 5:00, and 'tourigrinos' with light backpacks after that.

9/4/2004

trailside garden riot ~
    blackberry cascade
        fig leaves apple grapevine
            vine fern schist stonewall intertwine,
    impenetrable to sight, wind and rain.
        breathing
            beneath
                eucalyptus boughs,
            eyes nose throat shine.

9/4/2004

acorns and chestnuts
    thicken in cool September winds,
        fallen yellow leaves
    leave green twisted beans
        behind to haunt a weathered pole,
            ripe apple
                footfalls follow me,
heather sprig adorns walking staff
    walking through
        walking by
            being time.

journal - 9/5/04

powerful thunderstorms during and after salad pasta pizza wine with Ya-el last night. still flash and rumbling this morning. humid, mysterious, forested, passing showers, fog banks swallowing hills, more of the same crumbling agricultural hamlets...

the B & B in Santa Irene - crashed! throughout yesterday and today i'm experiencing waves of deep fatigue. hard to believe that tomorrow is the day, needing silence...

CCL and whiskey at the camp-like bar on the main drag to transcribe poems from scrap paper notes.

9/5/2004

bruise-blue storm
    clouds boil,
        thunder wanders southern sky
        on grasshopper lightening legs -
    low morning sun
        strikes green chestnut urchins,
            eucalyptus spice mist-pearl bedight -
red throated wren chirps,
    Jimmy sings 'ripple' down
        an ebbing trail.

9/5/2004

jungle humid morn,
    dawn-faint lightning fissures,
        thunder crackles roll -
    slender eucalyptus, oak and pine
            tickle low clouds, glean
        brume into aromatic mizzle,
                acorn snaps beneath

130 | James Timberlake

bootsteps sparking mind.
　　so many miles,
　　　　belly trembles,
　　　　　　eyes and sky rain.

9/5/2004

mystic crow rauks
　　muggy morning,
　　　　clouds blacken with dawn,
　　　　　　bright lightening dances
　　southern skies,
　　　　south wind rides thunder rolls ~

walking under canopy
　　of tree and vine i
　　　　only hear the rain ~

zazen folded cow herd
　　　　breathes canyon deep wind sounds
　　　　　　the other side of scythed back
　　　　　　　　blackberry brambles ~

far field pine and fern
　　bracken slowly vanish
　　　　in coming
　　fog-fall veils.

9/5/2004

　　　pause among
eucalyptus,
　　　　pine,
　　and boot-crushed wild mint ~
feeling
　　like a
　　　　cough drop.

journal - 9/8/04

two days ago - left Santa Irene at 4:am. scary. dark foggy pine and eucalyptus forests, winding trail. thinking of horror movies and those 'why did you go in there' fools. Ya-el said she left early as well. walked with some people who moved on at a quicker pace... and so left alone, she hid behind a rock until light spread!

the bridge into Santiago - fairly ugly outskirts. long walk through to the Casco Viejo - anticlimactic.

after getting a room in the pension on Plaza Galicia, showered and went out. in line for the Compostela at the Pilgrim's Office - everyone! Kristof, Miriam, Ya-el, Emmanuelle, Harry. bagged the hour wait and went to the Cathedral. bagged the Cathedral as well - too difficult after that mystic morning to be in the heart of the horde.

ran into Miriam, Katerina and Rudy at Café Barakal. Miriam had an awesome crock in front of her of shrimp swimming in garlic butter - everyone dunked. she walked from Munich and this was her 100th day away.

slept well, and late. woke to rain. a thundery morning.

emotional, ceremonial, processional mass... five guys in brown robes hauling on winch ropes swinging the incensor across the transept through the booming sounds of Organ.

great Italian restaurant. mozzarella and tomato salad / fish soup / carbonara and here i am, caught up. Mémère... my Grandmother is dying.

9/8/2004

       third day in Santiago,
          familiar trail-family
  faces fade
        into walking staffed,
      white-footed strangers
    embracing strangers ~ to each other dear.
the world in small becomes foreign again,
    thighs and arches ache
      to wander on westward
        to the sea.

journal - 9/10/04

morning stroll through stone streets. Arie the Dutch pastor is here with his wife who flew down from Holland to walk the last leg with him to Finisterre! he tells me he wrote an article in his church press about the SNEAKERS! i'm infamous in Holland.

there is something oceanic about the Cathedral. the lichen on the facade is the brownish yellow of seawrack - the gulls, the grey stone... an oceanside palatial feel.

journal - 9/11/04

up early and walked to the Cathedral just before 7:00. so silent, still, and low lit. went up to St. James, put my hands on his shoulders and stood there under the ornate Baroque gold dome, towering carved angels all around. this really is the shrine of James, his bejeweled statue is throned behind the altar and below the third steeple with a red presence light burning high like a 'one if by land two if by sea' lamp in the grey mist.

sat and meditated listening to walking stick tocks and soft whispers, bells ringing the quarter hours. with the third eye relaxed, a dream guide came to me in the form of a young tomcat on the streets of Santiago, a cat who kept looking at me, then moved around a corner without moving. feline litheness and curiosity and a sense of recognition.

mist, rain. with the long walk into Santiago proper i was surprised how quickly i walked out and back into old Galicia - down a road, over a bridge - into Ventosa - grapevines trellised close around homes. an old woman picking grapes and spatting out the sour seed-pulp offers me a bunch. stopped for a snack in Ponte Maceira. delicious setas à la plancha - pan crisped mushrooms dressed with crunchy garlic, parsley and olive oil.

Negreira was not far after. Arie and Clair! and Bruno! a couple Brazilians. no Spaniards. made lentils with onion, garlic, red pepper, zuchini and mushrooms from a well-stocked fruit and veg shop up on the corner...

9/11/2004

knowing Mémère
    will soon fade flesh
        and brighten setting suns to suns,
            i
    walk slow steps into
        St. James' palatial temple,
        bright doors open
        on the fog-wreathed hill,
    great sons of thunder bells
        tremble earth and sky.
            alone, but
            with one thousand years
                of pilgrims i
        lay hands
            upon the gold jeweled
                saint,

a friend of Jesus
in distant lands,
lay tau upon his
shoulder,
meditate in this frakensensed space,
listen to the song of whispers
with walking sticks tocking stone floor echoes,
fresh and weary pilgrims
in also awe.

9/11/2004

great sons of thunder bells
ring 8 o'clock,
three more days before
bathing in
the western sea
i walk out into wild Galician pathways
beneath eucalyptus,
mist and rain,
wading feet
in the mind stream.

9/11/2004

waking,
packing,
walking Santiago ochre
lamp-lit stone arcades, wet
granite slab streets
shine a special
silence.

eyes
    flesh
        breath
    dawn bright,
            walking in
            eucalyptus mist,
                rain patters,
                bird
            whistles wiggle ribbons
            through the trees, September
    ferns
                set forest floor
  a russet fire ~
  scythed stalk and cabbage rots'
      sour musk swims in the
      ripe purple scent of
each crumble stone
    Ventosa home's
        grapevine trellis
           shade.

journal - 9/12/04

dealing with 'don't want to be here' mind. overheard a couple French people yesterday saying they spent just one day in Santiago because more than that breaks the rhythm. disagreed inside then. agreeing in flesh now. thoughts of home, Mémère, not wanting to go home just for the funeral. don't think Mom was realistic saying it could be months away. no phone here. should have called last night.

left the albergue in Negreira about 7:30 and again stepped into the Galician past. mist, eucalyptus, fern... more forest floor dense with purple heather and gorse in yellow bloom. much ascent and

136 | James Timberlake

descent. after the highest of climbs the countryside changed - less eucalyptus, more oak and pine forests. a brinded cow herd coming down the trail.

skittish cats wanting nothing to do with me. serious peasants in rubber boots and aprons stiff-brushing out the cow-shat barn floor. old guy up high painting his hórreo, lemon verbena bush by his walkway. encountered more Taons today. vicious beasts, like Hell's Horseflies.

9/12/2004

birdsong echoes
        in foggy dawn,
    gentle resonations
            upon the brow ~
fire cloud fragments
            lick sky ~
        sweet September hay fermentation
            incenses mind ~
through vicious gorse thorns
        yellow gorse blooms
                constellate eucalyptus shade.

    journey's end
            a day away,
my family ebbs,
        sea bird cries
    splinter
            surf song
so far from
        the shore.

journal - 9/13/04

tossed often but rested well. such rural quietude in Olveiroa. last day jitters. foggy morning. stillness. trees lessen. gorse and heather, heather and gorse.

a day of the animals! at the bar near two belching smokestacks that clouded the sun for a while, at that bar in Hospital i was greeted by a friendly dog who soon got screech and whack-thumped by a car. seemed to shake it off and be alright. same bar - hazel-eyed siamese cat i fed cheese to from my bocadillo jumped up on my lap for a few minutes of purr and pet. later walking down the trail - freeze! what the hell is that beast charging towards!? a hare full-on bolting from a dog. dog stops at the sight of me. hare races right past stepping on my foot!

the steep descent... after all these many miles the first sight of the sea makes me simultaneously laugh and cry. blowing my nose a puppy comes panting up the trail, stops, rolls over for a belly and ear scratching then continues on.

made my way around the waterfront in Cee... up through steep neighborhoods, through eucalyptus and sun. Arie and Clair caught up with me. the Sneakers! or at least the story of the Sneakers have followed me from France to Finisterre. walked into the port with them along the boardwalked shore.

terrible heat rash. couldn't walk out to the peninsula this afternoon if i had wanted to. had soup with Miriam and Susan at the albergue. what's the word Susan used? a Greek Christian word for when the time is full and right? Kairos. Susan, Miriam and Kristof had their clothes burning ceremony on the beach today, and took a baptismal swim in the ocean. an annoying tourist taking objectifying pictures of 'pilgrims...' Miriam morphed into a banshee and chased her screaming back to her car.

9/13/2004

raw.
    still.
        white fog dawn shrinks
               vision to arm-lengths away,
        spiders pull
            dewy cotton tents
               among gorse and fern,
walking stick slices wisps from the air
    spinning eddies over
        silver grassy heights ~
behind,
    whitely
        waterly
            eddies spin into
    arm-breast cradling
            ancestors
        walking with me to the sea.
warm tear trickles chill
        through
            greying beard.

9/13/2004

walking through this
    white fog morn ~
            the 10,000 things
            appear from blue
        silhouette to
            precision,
               then fade.
purple heather dangling dew-pearls
        tremble at my footsteps,
    tranquil back
        to omphalos spheres.

9/13/2004

unzipped,
        pissing hot rain down,
           unseen grasshopper
      leaps for life,
   feeling bad but laughter rising,
        walking onward
           to the western sea.
fog swells
     drift valley below
  and through my morning shadow
     dew-jewels
       glisten grass,
     tears glisten lashes,
 and life born embrace
     embraces life through the brow and belly's eye.

journal - 9/14/04

woke to the smell of coffee. found a hostal as we're allowed only one night at the albergue. bought cheese, fruits, bread... and the time was slowly becoming full and right.

walked the 3K out to the cape collecting sticks and twigs. tour busses in sight. tourists photographing me. i looked away. scrambled down the rocks and spent five hours on the cliffs...

...walked back in the mist.

9/14/2004

pine-twig fire smoke
      haunts flesh   beard
            hair,
     settling into
       a quiet bar,
  iced whiskey clinking chiseled glass in hand
     ends ceremonials
       offered off
         the Finisterre cliffs ~

hunkered down on jagged stone shore
   to sip the sea
     from my cupped hand...
white-froth-wave-wall-thunder-death-fear
       crashes
       drenching me
leaping shouts and laughter to safety.
   with thumb i bless me
     in Celtic spirals,
       eternal ocean water streaming
       down Xacobean skin
  and rock-climb
     back to my chosen aerie...
       a place for ass and spine to ease against cliff stone,
to arrange tightly twisted El País pages
       and twigs into a bier
    for socks, for briefs, for t-shirt
        cremation,
  dwelling in the sound of waves ~

i rise,
    whip shoulderblade winging a
        long-carried scallop shell into the
            churning foam below,
    toss an apple there too to
        feed a sea god
    then fire my bier
transforming age-worn clothes
        into smoke.
standing folded hands above the flames
    on rugged cliff,
        between sea and cloud mist
veils
sending metta out to timelessness,
    the sound of surf
    and gull
        ignites
the city on the hill
    and pilgrimage
        into diurnal ways.

journal - 9/15/04

Miriam met me by the bus the next morning to wave me off. she's spending more time in Finisterre waiting for the universe to give her a sign as to what to do next.

in Santiago, much back-and-forthing to train station / bus station / internet bar, planning my way to a month-long retreat in Plum Village.

9/15/2004

long grey hair in
　　　sunlight shines,
　　wearing new, bright green
　　　　　pants to
　　　celebrate her new life's Spring
　　waiting for the universe to offer
　　　　　her golden guidance.
my friend Miriam,
　　Rosemary White Feet
　　　smiles heart-sky-wide smiles
waving ecstatic scarf in fresh sea air,
　　　sends me off to future ways
　　through the tinted bus window rumbling.

journal - 9/16/04

hung out in the Cathedral - met Valentino - a German pilgrim from southern Germany who left with no money and a guitar. helped him find the traditional free meal at Hostal dos Reis Católicos, and went shopping for warm clothes for the retreat. met Susan! the American hospitalera at Rabanal. i heard, "Hey, Justin's Brother!" and turn and there she was. she stayed with Jésus in Villafranca del Bierzo for a while and said he said his Mother used to say, 'even the guy who's a bit shifty IS God.' with tears in her eyes, a window to realization melts.

got an awesome haircut and beard trim. felt great to be groomed! went to the Barakal - my favorite place for shrimp swimming in garlic butter. love it. and here i sit, getting ready to sit... a lot! 2:30pm departure from Santiago, 5:30am arrival in Bordeaux. will find out once there how to get to Sainte-Foy-la-Grande.

journal - 9/16/04

screwed up the date at some point - 7:am next day and it's still the 16th. ? it was freakish to quickly pass Astorga, Ponferrada, and León. what took weeks on foot - all the people, food, visions, conversations - in six hours we were in Burgos!

biding my time in the Bordeaux bus station for the tourist office to open at 9:00. must find out if Sainte-Foy-la-Grande, where the monks pick up retreatants, is large enough to warrant continuing on there this morning.

found a hotel in Sainte-Foy - caretaking couple taking over for a while for her sister whose daughter is dying. sweet people - he's biking the Chemin from Le Puy in two weeks. gave him a pilgrim's cross... very excited to go.

hotly bathed in a deep deep tub.

salad of lettuce, walnut, Roquefort and lardons. carbonara came with an egg yolk sitting in its 1/2 shell among the farfalle for me to stir in.

journal - 9/17/04

had petit déj at the hotel - le monsieur showed me his itinerary and i told him about 'pince-sans-rire' M. Laberthe at Café la Commande, the Taberna Mateo, and the cool albergues in Astorga and Villafranca.

i see monks...

got in the van and went with them to the Leclerc department store for supplies, then through French countrysides and vineyards to

the Upper Hamlet of Plum Village capping a tree-enclosed hillish
outcropping.

9/17/2004

sun-striped shade,
        dry bamboo leaf fall
                crackles
        under cat lapping
    ass and balls.

9/18/2004

brow
    kisses
        ground
            timeless times,
    sangha transmission
        kneading inward beneath
            the skin,
saffron scarf draped brown robes rustle in candlelight,
        one boulder-sized bell baritones,
                closed lids ripple
            against near liquid eyes.
    opening to dawn...
        diving white-wing crow
                chases bat-out-o-hell cat
            across a Plum Village lawn.

9/19/2004

just a few
   moth-wing
      white and gold honeysuckle blooms,
  a few roses unfold
       against the stonewall,
  pink lotus buds unbind among
     ancestral seed pods
whose leathern leaves yellow, brown, and tear under time
   adding to the fertile swamp rot stew
   bright koi flash in,
        but just a few.
    a few brown robe monks
      walk wide smiles
  and softly feet falling
      by hard green persimmons
  bowing limbs.
blue sky clouds and rains,
  compassion brings the shoes i left out
    back under leeward meditation hall
     roof eaves.

9/20/2004

opening notebook to write,
  bell rings for lunch.

    Plum Village lazy day,
      morning conversation on infinity...
     bus stops between quantum leaps
     in bamboo wind,
   eyes follow bee across lawn
     to linden tree vanish.

146 | James Timberlake

in a ring of stone, wind nods
   orange dahlia
      yellow dahlia
         scarletest rose.

hoe   spade   wheelbarrow   earth
   scrap-wood 'n plastic...
      the Italian monk's herb
         garden dream slowly coalesces.
working with old Jim - "I shoot from the hip. Some people
   don't like me but I shoot from
   the hip."
   tattooed, goateed, 2-wived, alcoholic,
   8 years Friday without cigarette or weed.
     he heals here
       digging earth,
        "go wash
   your bowl o man"
           the immortals can only say.

trading places with another
   a boy-monk drives
   John Deere over hummock
      mowing stones!
    shredding metal and granite shards
       clatter to a big green stop ~
sudden Star Wars Jawa robes running towards,
   flutter little hands fidget   prod
    fiddle   poke   rock and   lift
   someone unlatch-flips open the engine
     panel...
sitting apart from the pack
   on a stump, shaking his head,
     fresh shorn scalp sheen
   young black American monk

lips, cheekbones, lashes over
   ebony eyes
manifestly working with frustration,
"It's not the MOTOR
   man, he slammed into a ROCK.
   The blades are jammed."
shaking sheen head in hand
   apart from the pack
     sitting on a stump...
   brown robes go their separate ways.
 the John Deere lists in silence
between sunset and tumbling leaves.

sweet harmonia,
   sixty-guys-chewing-in-silence song,
     arrhythmic rhythm.
   sixty mindful spoons against sixty bowls
   and the silence
     7 o'clock rung brings
   tides meal time.

in Transformation Meditation Hall
one giant dragonfly clatters
   shellacked wings against
 bright window
   between my helping hands horror
   and the jewel of obsession sun.

Brother Gilles' near whisper, "Do you still
   want to come?"
 then and now tumbles
   into always and
i squat hillside
   in ochre late day light,
     slowly swim arm motions
       gathering

148 | James Timberlake

fallen powder-indigo
    plums,
gathering glowing sun-warm fruit off the
    cosmic ground
for Plum Village
    jam.
        breath and fingers
        smelling of plum wine
            where
    then and now
        tumble into always.

journal - 9/21/04

last night's stick counting ceremony. there were levels of lay and monastics who would attend all 90 days of the Rain Retreat. one monk went down the aisles dispensing colored sticks from a tray, one monk behind him collecting the sticks which were then counted and the number of attendees was reported. this is a closed retreat and during the ceremony the boundaries of the monastery were established for the three month period... this oak row / that farm / this road / on Thursday and Sunday the road to the nun's Lower Hamlet may be walked upon to attend Dharma talks.

in this morning's opening ceremony each of the above groups lined up, knelt down, and a representative had a formal back and forth conversation with the Elders that they were committed to deepening their practice in the Sangha for the entire retreat - this was after many prostrations before the many names and manifestations of the Buddha.

Deep Relaxation. feel the whole body bottom out against the earth. feel supported by the earth. feel the breath. allow breath to deepen and massage the lower belly. start from the top of the head and relax all the way down... relax the eyes and the energy of sight, relax the length of spine and all the many braided muscles, the long muscles in the legs, around the knees, shins, calves, ankles, arches, toes. and then through the breath dwell in the whole body with relaxed awareness. start reinvigorating from the toes wiggling all the way back up to a vigorous face massage.

meditative sign at eyelevel on the toilet... "defiled or immaculate / increasing or decreasing / these concepts exist only in our mind / the reality of interbeing is unsurpassed."

9/21/2004

eyes closed in
    bamboo rustle
       grove,
waiting for brown robed
    monk to bow to bat,
awaken bell for dinner time
    and still monastery-wide action,
       listening with everyone to deep resonations
          fade.

journal - 9/22/04
Thich Nhat Hanh - before today's meditation:

"I am sitting with my Father.
    I am sitting with my Mother.
       I am sitting with my Teacher.
    Peace and Happiness are within me.
       I am sitting with my Brothers and Sisters and Friends.
       Peace and Happiness are within me.
          I breathe.

Inside, I have arrived.
I breathe.
Outside, I am home.
I breathe,
and each breath is nourishing."

fluctuations in the schedule as they're getting in the mode for the Three Month Retreat. because the monks are renewing the Ten Mindfulness Trainings after breakfast, i was asked to work in the pre-lunch kitchen.

Thây's calligraphy - "the bread in your hand is the body of the cosmos." and "drink your tea."

the Italian brother is funny. when Robert was picking at the potatoes i fried for tonight's dinner he came over and said to him, "Thank you very much for your help. (deep bow) Now go!"

9/22/2004

in Plum Village shimmer light,
my slant shadowed legs are cool,
torso sweats with radiant warmth ~
'tis fall.
wringing basin-washed clothes out,
Finisterre cliff firesmoke lingers
in wet shirt and pants' weave.
pitchfork turned sharp compost waft.
a neighbor's bleating lamb...
wet chafed knuckles
glisten sun beads
and thoughts flash
to Gramma Timberlake,
now dust dew sun rain cleome
geranium lemon verbena chinese
evergreen red berry bright

Upon This Stoney Holy Year | 151

jewel in me,
remembering to me her Mother...
    "Poor Mother."
a Great-Grandmother i never knew
    hanging wet clothes on the clothesline,
        winter steam
            rolling off thick
                Polish matron arms,
      "Poor Mother."
thoughts dwell,
      "Poor Mother."
        i've only ever seen one
            photo of her and my morning
    mirror...
    "Poor Mother."
man's eyes tear
    to hear in mind Gramma's
        chanting storytelling voice
           "Poor Mother."
    time's bloom's dew.

journal - 9/23/04
Thây's opening meditation words:

"Mother, I know you are with me,
    in every cell of my body you are with me.
    I am your continuation in the same way the corn plant
    is the continuation of the corn.
Father... when I breathe, when I smile, you breathe and smile.
    You may not have had the opportunity to be still
    but we can be still now together
    and find the peace, joy, tranquility and happiness
        of being in the present moment."

first Dharma talk - abiding / dwelling / taking refuge in the peace and happiness of the Here and Now. concentration on 'refuge' as something more than a nice idea. to actually take true refuge in the present moment and not be caught by the past or the future - mind and body aligned in concentrated awareness.

went on to talk about the sectarian divisions after the Buddha's death - how the Mahayana texts were invented 300-600 years later, but this didn't matter since the Sutras reflect impermanence, no-self, and nirvana - the Three Seals. how immediately after the Buddha's death Buddhism spread to 20 countries but died out because the Dharma teachers were using the same old rant and not adopting nontraditional subjects to teach Buddhism. since it didn't resonate it died out.

things to make they make here:

plum syrup. i think this is just the excess liquid from making plum jam. so good spooned over oatmeal.

breakfast delights - oatmeal and quinoa, Muselix, sunflower seeds and hot milk.

really like the bitter melon soup - a shocker the first time i had a huge bowl of it. good for the liver 'they' say.

condiment - sunflower seeds and peanuts food-processed with dried chilis.

look up Master Linji - IXth Century China.

journal - 9/24/04
Thây today:

"Dear Buddha,
    I know you are not on the altar
        but within me in every
        cell of my body.
    When I smile, you smile.
        When I breathe, you breathe."

9/24/2004

ass warms cushion,
    hands warm thighs,
        shins warm mat,
    mind burns behind closed eyes ~
        now,
            one silken sun-lit
        bat tumbles palm
           fronds, cricket
           chortles,
    and clear moonlight falls.

journal - 9/25/04
Thây today:

"Lord Buddha - when I see a leaf I know the leaf is breathing, I know the leaf is using the sun and air to make sap to nourish itself and the whole tree. And I do the same."

"When I breathe I nurture my Mother and my Father who are within me and around me; my ancestors and my spiritual ancestors who are within me and around me; my Brothers, Sisters, and

Friends who are within me and around me; and my Children who are within me and around me."

"I am the continuation, and I am continued, and Lord Buddha I breathe for you."

9/25/2004

brilliant
    sunset,
        even the green
            bamboo is gold.
    pine cone, needle tuft, rough branch silhouette.

journal - 9/26/04
Thây today:

"Lord Buddha, when I breathe in I feel I have arrived.
    When I breathe out I feel I am home
        and all the wonders of the Kingdom of God and
        the Pure Land of the Buddha are available to me.
            I have been running
            for many lifetimes,
    now when I stop, and breathe,
    and arrive, all my ancestors
        arrive with me
            and there is freedom."

first Dharma talk was in Vietnamese - historical. the split after the Buddha's death into progressives and classicists - then and now, throughout time, and here in this Plum Village Sangha - how both are branches on the same tree. dry. for the second Dharma talk i was washing dishes. had to laugh. the thought arose - all this way to wash dishes - BAM! the epitomal classic exchange between novice and master. if i can't learn it here at the sink i don't belong in the meditation hall.

journal - 9/27/04
posted on the reading room door -

"Entering the meditation hall
    I see my true mind.
        I vow that once I sit down
            all disturbances will stop."

a lazy day throughout Plum Village. scheduled non-activity. slept in until 6:30 - and it's a beautiful day for a walk to Sigoulès.

9/27/2004

deep night piss,
    hoot owl mimes
        bright moon,
    thin fog
leaves behind
        rain's allure
    on dark
        pearl dewed ground -
here,
    in morning meditation
        i hear carmel
            whiskey ice cubes
        clinking chiseled tumbler sides
a misty six-kilometer walk away.

9/27/2004

between Sigoulès and Pomport
    a narrow path shortcuts through
        hilly woods and
    vineyard's
            rose-adorned rows.
    by one pine tucked
        wild fig tree
    i peel royal purple
        fruit to white flesh perfection
and invisible glory unfolds
    behind lips,
        teeth, tongue,
            mind ~
    low pond duck flock
        laughs at me,
            the shortening
                September days.

9/27/2004

Plum Village
    softly clacking bamboo
        grove Dharmas ~
i break
    soya, rice and raw veg
        wind ~
the two white chairs
    where two brown-robed monks
        sat last night to
    watch the bright moon
            are gone.

9/27/2004

slip soft shoes on,
   dimmer lightswitch down,
     door dance
  into bright moon
      cricket-dom.

journal - 9/28/04

didn't hear the bell this morning. few in the room did. all the
monastics were down at the Lower Hamlet spending the day with
Thây alone.

9/28/2004

limb
  leaf
    universal oaken sky...

long bass-pipe wind-chimes
  echo within their metal.
    my hammock,
      by occasional stick-to-trunk invitations
    swings smoothly.
leg to leg and
arms to torso
    are enough
      to keep warm comfort
    under the late September
      oaken limb-leaf dome.
    at odd moments,
  acorns swole with Kairos
    drop,
  knock knock knocking 'who's there?'
    upon the earth.

journal - 9/29/04
Thây this morning:

"I see the Tathagata,
    the fully enlightened one,
        in every cell of my being,
    enjoying the miracles of this life."

entered the Hall this morning - 5:30 - beautifully clear. left at 6:15
- beautifully foggy. and the full moon shines above.

9/29/2004

soothe long early-
    morning meditation ~

full moon phosphorescent
    forestral exhale,
        through flowing fogs
            softly
        walking
            back
    to squeal door stone walls...
to sleeping bag, cot and heater
        nestled,
    dream wading waiting
        in dark room
    for breakfast mallet to
        meet breakfast bell,
            echoeing another
                monastery dawn.
another revolution round
        another evolution by
    another star,
            conscious
        of the holy indigo
                star field
    sky.

9/29/2004

watching
   Thây's feet
      in walking meditation...
      supple ankle
         heel hover
      over earth
   before there planting mind ~
      yellow
   buttercup has learned
      to bloom
below
   the mower's
      blade.

9/29/2004

full moon
   meditation,
      steeped in
         yin ~
   invisible koi
nips lotus stem,
   lotus bead-seeds'
      dry pod rattles
         against cool night.
silver wind and
   silver water
      rippling.

journal - 9/30/04
Thây:

"Tathagata, World Honored One - when I breathe in I see my Father, Mother, and Teacher in me. Not as an image, but as a complete reality because I am their continuation. They are available to me and I to them because I can stop and look deeply."

long dry Dharma talk in Vietnamese. more... actually i'm wondering if it's a style of mnemonic teaching. it seems now there have been three Dharma talks with the same topic - divisions after the Buddha's death, etc. but each one is slightly fuller, more thorough, and slightly different.

walking meditation through orchard and woods, everyone plucking blackberries. i skipped the formal lunch and whatever meetings ensued and walked back to nap in the quiet hamlet. i like retreats. i dislike 'group.'

last night's dreams - hearing footsteps behind and turning around... a tall dark caped figure stood in the wind at a 3/4 shoulder stance to me, staring. dark purplish face and scarified, no hat, not hooded - didn't feel threatened. actually noted i felt calm. can't remember the exchange we had but it was well elocuted - Brontë style - that i should be aware of the wolves and dangers. later in dream village i told an old woman about this and in her expression it was as if i had met something out of legend.

9/30/2004

Plum Village
    Lower Hamlet
        apple orchard
            in
        serious need of pruning.

plump purple
    udder-hung grapevine
        rows
        guide eyes to
September
    weathered-grey
        sunflower seedhead
          field
        staring groundward.

chestnut
    bloom by bee,
        sun,
        rain, earth, gene, time...
        green sea-urchin burr
          burst
            open upon
cool ground
            births sheen-wood-shelled
nut to sky.

journal - 10/1/04
Thây:

"Even though it is dark outside I know the cherry tree is there. The sun will rise, bees and butterflies will appear. Breathing in, I am aware I am alive. Breathing out, I smile to all life and am present for the cherry tree, the bees, butterflies, my ancestors, my Brothers and Sisters and my Children, and they are present for me."

10/1/2004

after early morning meditation,
   dark path walking woods,
      a pause.
         one sunless bee's lost wings
           vibrato
  fog,
          a beaded leaf patters.
     glad the piss
       is finished and the
          tenderest is tucked
away.

10/1/2004

Plum Village
   tea room,
      reading Ryōkan, mind thrashes
         in sudden raftless sea ~
  entering Transformation Meditation Hall
        two flies leave,
     resident tabby stops mid-ass lick,
        pours paw patters across carpet
          to share a flea, my heat,
  and finger time ~
through broad windows
   always one yellow leaf wobbles
      time-of-her-life free
   down to the raked grass ground ~
mange monastery hound
      nods three breeze sniffs,
   plops head back down
     upon earth's belly
       in linden shade.

10/2/2004

cat eyes
    breathing stillness
        over mole holes,
      palmed
        hot bowl of tea
      reflects the bamboo tattered sky.

everyone at Plum Village
    has fleas.
    everyone at Plum Village disguises deeply scratching their
      hairy V's
        by seemingly deep pocket
        shifting shorts
      beneath baggy pants or
        brown robes.

Thây,
    the sun my heart -
      this Interbeing sucks.

journal - 10/4/04

using Anders' dream technique of 'imagine your childhood
bedroom closet - the door you never saw before there opens - the
steep staircase down to a stream - the boat - the drift to a sandy
shore - the tree you sit beneath where you relax and begin to
dream...

enjoyed the walk to Sigoulès. enjoyed being away.

10/4/2004

       Sigoulès,
between 12:00 and 12:05,
        église St. Jacques le Majeur's belfry
       bangs out angelus and time ⁓
one man's shuffling
   feet V a praying mantis
       safely across Rue de la Mayade ⁓
yellow leaves hang
      above the brown leaved ground.

10/4/2004

Plum Village dining hall clock
     rings the hour on the hour
         stilling steps and mindful chews
     to breathe and by breath connect
   with an ultimate miracle or two.
      said Bob,
even the cat paused paws ⁓

mange monastery dog
   wanting deep eye contact
   'o man read my handout hunger and
     my happy wagging tail,'
   sniffing seated sandals and
       brown robe hems ⁓
out the window behind oaks,
   sun plays flicker
      shower o' gold god
        with green leaves ⁓

clock, cat, Bob,
    dog, robe, sun.
        dear Mémère slowly leaving
            us and her embraced life
        behind on my mind.
    in the vineyard ribbed
        haze-blue morning valley
        below
i know a quiet road
    to softly walk sweet elegies.

10/4/2004

dirt track between
    vineyard and wood,
        eating Grand Jury taboulé oriental
and Pierre Martinet, 'Le traiteur intraitable,'
        salade de lentilles aux oignons émincés
          out their plastic boxes
        with a chocolate bar's blue cardboard
          wrapper
        folded into a spoon.
strewn lime green chestnut burrs
    envy my meal and i
        chew for songbirds
          whose diet i do not crave ~
days away a plane awaits.
        so much to leave.
        so much to return to.
    sitting
    eating
    breathing honey tinted late-day breeze...
        now
this light purple cornflower field,
    this light purple haze
        butterflies dye dusty wings in.

10/4/2004

comme les paysans d'antans
   et les
      moines de ces jours-ci,
         i'm feeling like a Jean-François Millet
  painted canvas
      pitching hay
      onto a tarp to pull and pile
        nearer the compost cage,
hearing frenzied bees' wings
  swan for all diminishing flowers,
    all swelling fruit and seeds,
      for all lengthening chill night hours,
  for Mémère's dying dreams.

      walking softly back,
        crows brocade a
  broken fence.
   'jeezum christopher
      they got big pigeons
      in France.'

journal - 10/5/04

walking meditation out to the oaks. sitting on a low elbowed oak branch moving with the warm wind, looking out over the fields and Peyguilhem.

helped clean up the recycling midden with Br. Lúc. helped Jim haul pallets. helped try to move the blue wasp-infested brokedown van but the steering wheel was locked.

hubbub at Plum Village. Vietnamese dignitaries and Venerables are coming tomorrow to formally invite Thây to Vietnam after over 30 years of exile!

10/5/2004

slender slight breasted
  young asian beauty
    snips bamboo sprigs
  to heighten floral sprays
      adorning
        tomorrow's visiting
        Vietnamese Venerables' and Dignitaries'
  eyes,
    those formally inviting Thây
      back homeland
        to teach
      where the word has gone
        form stale ~
monastery cat soft
  belly breathes a
    dry late-day golden
    bamboo leaf nest nap ~
cosmos ripples
  then stills at my lips
    in a spiced milky bowl of tea.

10/5/2004

sun sets.
  i make my darkening way
  back to an afternoon oak
    that meant the smiling world to me
      seated on a low limb... bright day shade,
        field slopes, pines, vineyards,
          tilled-earth hills hiding
  th' horizon away...
        butterfly wings flap thousand-mile winds.

168 | James Timberlake

in now's dark oak-groved rustling heights
　　　nursing warm evening October air,
　　　　　thousand-mile winds rock my limb,
　　　　　meditation's cradle.
　　phantom ancestor footsteps stroll
　　　in falling acorn guise.

　　watching
　　　the stars
　　　　between
dark leaves.

journal - 10/6/04
Thây:

"Tathagata,
　　you teach 'The past is no longer there,
　　　and the future is not yet here.'
　　　　Now is the only moment in which we live.
　　Breathing in, I have arrived.
　　Breathing out, I feel I am home.
　　　Breathing in - solid.
　　　Breathing out - free.
　　Breathing in, I am aware of life.
　　Breathing out, I touch the miracles of life.
Solidity and Freedom form the ground for experiencing
　　the treasure of the Pure Land in the Here and Now."

journal - 10/7/04

two Dharma talks - first, again, concerning the splits after the
Buddha's death. i think there were words directed at the 'old

school' Venerables about their conservatism. second DT was about the inner child suffering in oneself and in all people.

liked what Thây said about the 'I have arrived' being not a statement, but the realization of intention.

spent the last two nights teaching the first movement of Dragon and Tiger to Anders and Ben. i'd forgotten how soothing and softening doing just that opening form really is.

journal - 10/8/04
Thây:

"Breathing in and breathing out...
    Being aware of my life and that I am surrounded by life
            IS
        enlightenment."

this morning... meditation, nap, breakfast, packed, hung out in the bamboo grove, then took off in the van. the only train to Lyon, (due East), is via Paris, (due North). and i haven't been to Paris in quite some time! even in 2002, when my vacation overlapped with Mom and Dad's, we had less time there than i thought - would love to find our restaurant - Auberge de la Jarente - and go again.

found a hotel near the departure station - Gare de Lyon. walked smiling through the bustling St-Germain-des-Prés quarter. the Highlander Pub - no one speaks French! 20$ for a Jack Daniels and a Beamish stout!

journal - 10/9/04

cool overcast Parisian morning. the Marais. found la Jarente!
bowel emergency. nearly lost it on the Métro. at Montmartre a
Vendages, (harvest), festival going on! wines, spices, sausages,
breads, honey, rain. on the café-ringed plaza below Sacré Coeur -
writing postcards, watching parades... someone singing:

Chevaliers de la table ronde,
Goûtons voir si le vin est bon.
Chevaliers de la table ronde,
Goûtons voir si le vin est bon.
Goûtons voir, oui oui oui,
Goûtons voir, non non non,
Goûtons voir si le vin est bon.

now at la Jarente - before me chorizo and squid in a tomato
and pepper stew. delicious piperade. crisp confit de canard with
potatoes cooked in duck fat and sautéed wild mushrooms. et le
vin est bon!

10/9/2004

hair   brow
    eyes
            cheeks
    go pallid.
        Paris metro cold sweat
            panic ~

    morning coffee
        meets
    evening meal.
sphincter
    losing
        ground.

Upon This Stoney Holy Year | 171

journal - 10/10/04

strolled to Notre Dame just in time for full bell eruption below grey buttresses, grey skies, tannic brown chestnut leaves and the 10:am Gregorian Mass.

Musée d'Orsay. fell in love with Odilon Redon and out with much of sweetly soft Monet. practicing soft sight looking at the paintings and seeing what emerges. much more engaging than glaring at them. soft sighting reveals the general shapes the painter played with to create the images. the Millet peasants - coclicots and the gently trod path through them. parasoled women on the windy hill. new appreciation for Degas' dancers. Rousseau's snake charmer. van Gogh's everything! especially the writhing blue sky-wrapped church.

Auberge au Vieux Paris - dark wood and candles, heavy fabric on tables, heavy drapes, heavy cutlery, Laguiole knives from the Aveyron region! there is a stylized lowly prancing horse figurine to hold the knife up off the table. went down to the wine cellar to select my own dusty bottle from the racks. house cured ham. snails in crème fraîche, garlic and bread crumbs baked in a casserole. almost had the steak from Aubrac - flashback to Maurice in Navarrenx when the topic turned spiritual... "Le boeuf - voilà mon inspiration!" with beef blood dripping off the lip. wonder if he ever made it... wonder how his 'mule' fared? decided on another confit de canard with ratatouille and duck fat roasted potatoes.

10/10/2004

Notre 10-ton Dame
   bells
ripple noon down dark
   Seine,
      the cloud dim sky,
     tannin-gold chestnut leaves
       tremble whispers beyond time,
knowing Plum Village mind pauses
   i pause in Parisian wind
     and smile.

journal - 10/11/04

apéritif - compari and white vermouth on crushed ice with an orange. ordered a Croque Provinçal for lunch.

Luxembourg Gardens were alluring in a fading flower garden kind of way. after absorbing it all on the White Chairs for a while i made my way through Saint-Germain-des-Prés, the Louvre grounds, loving the general activity up Boulevard de l'Opéra. since last night i've been wanting to buy some Laguiole knives for a family gift and snap! there's a store. i'll deal with the credit card later.

looking up at a Red Neon Marquee - "Ian Anderson plays Jethro Tull!" with the frikin' Prague Philharmonic! i love Paris.

journal - 10/12/04

the 12th is upon me. arose, paid, left. train to Lyon. the several hotels by the Gare are full and i didn't stay at the Athens as planned. should have reserved 3 1/2 months ago! walked toward the center through the North African quarter and finally saw the historic Lyon! there must be four arrondissements all embraced by UNESCO - beautiful!

enjoyed the concert last night. Ian was so cool, relaxed, doing what he does, no pretense... 'Hot Night in Budapest' backed up by a full orchestra!

as i have only gross plane food to look forward to i'll chow now. aubergine, sundried tomato, tomato, tuna, artichoke heart, roasted pepper antipasto. this 2001 Bonera is tasty too. i'll be home tomorrow by 7:30pm. keep it alive, Jimmy. keep it alive.

10/12/2004

urban café canopy conversation stew.
    over coffee and iced whiskey,
        rain cloud black duck
    silhouette silent flies.

Paris-to-Lyon wide TGV window ride ~
    valley castle,
        goat-herd field,
            haybale columned stable,
    woods i know a stoney trail
            runs through,
hamlet chimney smokes Mary Poppin's
    stairway to the horizon away.

no muck shit scent,
    no malt grain ferment,
        no woodsmoke sparks nose,
no bootsteps grind, nor walking staff
    tocks pace beneath starry time,
    and i can hardly hear this train's wheel-rail song.

pilgrim days end,
    Frodo steps upon
        an elven westbound barque.

6/24/2004

after pilgrim's mass,
    Le Puy Bishop's blessing
        around the statue of St. James.
he, a few slow kind words
    after each spoke their place of origination,
often lost in old Cathedral stone echoes,
    but what is breathed kind remains...
candles flicker into stillness
    as centuries of wax-wick flame
        have here
before the Road to Santiago's
    fears and joys and pains express soul sweat flesh.

from much mind wandering and wondering how...
    wind and incense spark now's lips.
these early morning cobblestone steps,
    walking stick ticking beside me,
        dawn behind.